THE RESPONSE

JAMES GOLDSMITH

THE RESPONSE

MACMILLAN

First published 1995 by Macmillan
an imprint of Macmillan General Books
25 Eccleston Place London SW1W 9NF
and Basingstoke

Associated companies throughout the world

ISBN 0 333 66512 0

987654321

A CIP catalogue record for this book is available from
the British Library.

Printed and bound in Great Britain by Rede Design Limited

Contents

Acknowledgements

My thanks for their advice, research and help to
Claudie Broyelle, Jacques Broyelle, Jon Cracknell,
Bruno Erhard-Steiner, Charles Filmer,
Allegra Huston, Claude Henry Leconte,
Bridget Morrison, Loretta Roccanova.

Foreword

The English version of my book *The Trap* was published in November 1994, a little over a year after it first appeared in French. The second chapter, 'The New Utopia: GATT and Global Free Trade', attracted considerable adverse comment, including a European Commission document handed for information to the British press and a booklet published by the Centre for Policy Studies in the series *The Rochester Papers*. Most of the other comments appeared in columns or reviews in the British press of either the French or the British edition.

I have regrouped the principal criticisms into eight chapters, quoted the most significant and answered them.

The full text of the relevant chapter of *The Trap* is reproduced for easy reference as an appendix. The illustrated story of global free trade, using charts, begins on page 121.

James Goldsmith

The Critics

The European Commission, in a document handed for information to the British press on 18 October 1994.

The Right Honourable Chris Patten, Governor of Hong Kong, in a speech to the Swiss Bank Corporation and its guests on 27 October 1994.

Dr Brian Hindley, Co-Director of the Trade Policy Unit of the Centre for Policy Studies and Senior Lecturer in Economics at the London School of Economics, in a pamphlet 'The Goldsmith Fallacy: Why open trade and Gatt are best', published as *Rochester Paper 3* by the Centre for Policy Studies, December 1994.

Norman Macrae, former Deputy Editor of the *Economist* and currently a columnist for the *Sunday Times,* in two articles in the *Sunday Times*: 'Rebirth of the Great Protection Racket', 6 November 1994, and 'Trading Places', 12 December 1994.

Professor John Kay, Chairman of London Economics and Professor of Economics at the London Business School, in an article in the *Daily Telegraph*, 'The mercantilist fallacy must not entrap free trade', 28 December 1994.

Tim Congdon, Managing Director of Lombard Street Research, in an article in *The Times,* 'Goldsmith's closed book', 18 November 1994.

Paul Goodman, columnist in the *Sunday Telegraph,* in an article in the *Sunday Telegraph*, 'Protectionism is no protection', 6 November 1994.

1

How conventional economists misinterpret Ricardo.

Chris Patten, speech to the Swiss Bank Corporation,
27 October 1994:

'Sir James, however, sees in Adam Smith . . . and the Ricardian theory of trade, ideas which are no longer relevant to our world and its ways.'

' . . . money [moves] round in a world increasingly free of exchange controls. If money, I'm inclined to enquire deferentially, why not mutton and socks?'

Brian Hindley, 'The Goldsmith Fallacy':

'Ricardo's comparative cost theory, though 180 years old, still presents the principal intellectual obstacle to the attempt of Sir James, et al., to move from the observation that the world is changing to the conclusion that the EU should cut itself off from the world.' *

---

* Of course, I have never suggested that 'the EU should cut itself off from the world'. My recommendation is that we replace global trade agreements with bilateral agreements that satisfy the fundamental objectives of both contracting parties.

THE RESPONSE

Some ideas, indeed, are no longer relevant The world has changed. Capital and technology have become instantaneously transferrable. Goods can be manufactured anywhere in the world to be sold anywhere else. A communications and technological revolution is in progress. All this, along with the fall of communist ideology and the shift in the economic and political systems of many socialist and corporatist countries, has enabled 4 billion people from the ex-Soviet Union, China, India, Bangladesh, Eastern Europe and many other nations to enter the free world's economy (see Chart 1, page 123).[1]

Ricardo's theory, expounded in 1817, is based on the belief that feelings of community keep capital at home. He writes:

> Experience, however, shews, that the fancied or real insecurity of capital, when not under the immediate control of its owner, together with the natural disinclination which every man has to quit the country of his birth and connexions, and intrust himself with all his habits fixed, to a strange government and new laws, checks the emigration of capital. These feelings, *which I should be sorry to see weakened*, induce most men of property to be satisfied with a low rate of profits in their own country, rather than seek a more advantageous employment for their wealth in foreign nations.[2] [emphasis added]

THE RESPONSE

If capital is immobile, a nation's production is limited by the extent of its own capital and other resources. It is because of the limitation of capital that a nation can benefit by concentrating its limited capital on the production of goods in which it has a comparative advantage.

On the other hand, if capital is mobile, funds can flow in unlimited quantities to whatever country provides the highest rate of return on investment. Under such circumstances it is possible, in theory, for a group of countries to take over the production of an overwhelming proportion of the world's output of goods. Thus, instead of being shared between nations on the basis of comparative advantage, economic activity is shifted wholesale to those regions which have an absolute advantage, in other words an advantage which applies across a broad range of manufactured goods and services. (This is one of the reasons why mobility of capital is different from mobility of 'mutton or socks'.)

Today, capital is being transferred to the developing world in massively increasing amounts. In the period 1989–92, the average capital transferred per year to emerging countries was 116 billion dollars. In 1993, the figure was 213 billion dollars and in 1994 it was an estimated 227 billion dollars.[3] East Asia leads the field, with a rise in the annual rate of direct investment between 1984 and 1994 of 1100 per cent (see chart on next page).[4]

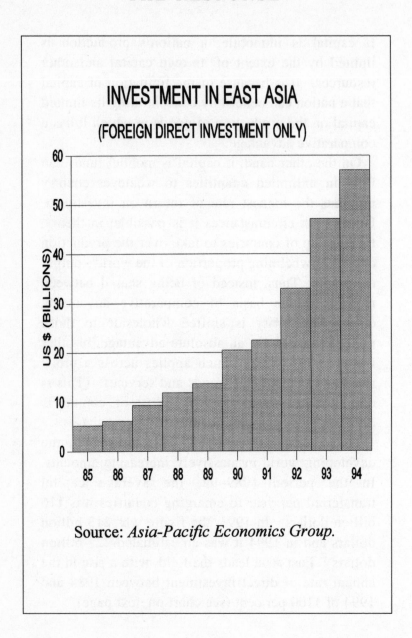

INVESTMENT IN EAST ASIA
(FOREIGN DIRECT INVESTMENT ONLY)

Source: *Asia-Pacific Economics Group*.

When the same technology is available but labour in one country costs more than forty times less than in another (see Chart 2, page 125), the sharing of value-added between capital and labour is radically altered. And the consensus that emerged painfully in the West, as a result of strikes, lockouts and political debate, is shattered.

To benefit from these new conditions, capital is transferred by transnational corporations to cheap-labour countries to finance modern factories and to equip them with state-of-the-art technology. These factories will produce goods to be sold in the markets of the developed nations, thus destroying jobs at home.

That is how two parallel economies with conflicting interests have been created – the corporate economy and the national economy. Corporate profits rise as personal earnings and employment fall.

A further substantial change in the way the world economy functions is the volatility of currency exchange rates. Comparative advantage, necessarily, must be calculated in money terms.[5] If a product costs X pounds sterling to manufacture in the UK and Y US dollars in America, all you need to do is to convert dollars into sterling at the going rate of exchange and it will be clear where the product is cheapest to manufacture and, therefore, where the comparative advantage lies. But if the rate of exchange is transformed by a devaluation or a revaluation of one of the currencies, then the relative costs change accordingly. Between 1981 and 1985, the value of the US dollar, for example, doubled against many European currencies. Between 1985 and 1995 it halved. So a product which in 1981, at the then ruling rate of exchange, cost the same to manufacture in the US as in the hard-currency European nations, had by 1985 become twice as expensive to produce in the US. Leading European nations suddenly acquired a comparative advantage. During the following ten years the Europeans lost this advantage as the value of the dollar sank.

Yet, according to Ricardian theory, each nation is supposed to specialize in those products in which it has a comparative advantage. If you followed this reasoning, you would have concentrated on industries in America which had a comparative advantage in 1981 but you would have had to abandon them in 1985. The rise in the value of the dollar would have eliminated the advantage. And industries on which you might have concentrated in Europe in 1985 would have had to be abandoned by 1995 as a result of the rise in the value of the European currencies. In both cases, industries would have come and gone purely as a consequence of currency fluctuations.

John Maynard Keynes, said, 'I sympathize, therefore, with those who would minimize, rather than with those who would maximize, economic entanglement between nations. . . . let goods be homespun whenever it is reasonably and conveniently possible, and above all, let finance be primarily national.'[6]

2

Protection and its role in the economic emergence of the United States, the nations of the European Economic Community, Japan and the newly industrialized countries.

John Kay, Daily Telegraph, *28 December 1994:*

'But [Goldsmith's argument] is an old story. It has been told for a hundred years or more and it has always proved wrong. It is contradicted empirically by the inescapable fact that the world has grown steadily richer over the period in which world trade has been liberalized. The nations that have grown richer most quickly have been the ones – like the newly industrialized countries of South-East Asia – that have participated in that growth of world trade.

The only countries that have actually become poorer are those, like some African and South American regimes, which have set their face against free trade.'

Tim Congdon, The Times, *18 November 1994:*

'It was because the US and Continental European countries did not support free trade that the 1930s witnessed a global trading catastrophe.'

The European Commission, document of 19 October 1994:

'For all economies, therefore, access to the global market is an essential precondition for sustained economic growth.'

Professor Murray Weidenbaum, former Chairman of the Council of Economic Affairs of the US, in the San Diego Union, *30 April 1985:*

'In the 1930s, protectionist measures contributed substantially to worldwide depression.'[1]

Paul Goodman, Sunday Telegraph, *6 November 1994:*

'But the cost [of protection] – inflation, uncompetitiveness, state intervention – ensures defeat in the long run.'

Norman Macrae, Sunday Times, *12 December 1994:*

'Still, as a practical man, Goldsmith might ponder that his proposed system . . . was that which operated in the Communist bloc from 1945 to 1990.'

THE RESPONSE

Professor Kay is wrong when he repeats the conventional view that, unlike some African and South American nations, the newly industrialized countries (NICs) embraced the liberalization of world trade. Rather, the two largest, Taiwan and South Korea, took advantage of open markets while carefully protecting their own home markets. (Taiwan and South Korea are countries with a combined population of 66 million people; the other two NICs, Singapore and Hong Kong, are city-states with a combined population of 8.7 million people.)[2]

During the Cold War, the US was willing to grant major privileges to nations which it saw as useful allies against communism. The NICs, strategically placed to help contain China, North Korea and Vietnam, were granted liberal access to the world's richest markets without being required to liberalize their own. They exploited this opportunity to the full by using their cheap labour, importing technology, encouraging export-oriented industry and regulating their currencies. Massive exports and controlled imports resulted in a historic transfer of wealth from the West to the NICs which represents one of the greatest subsidies granted to allied nations during any war. (See Appendix A to this chapter for further information.)

At a time when the World Bank, the International Monetary Fund and GATT were all condemning restrictions on the free flow of goods, the NICs were able to use their protected local markets as a springboard to conquer market share in the world economy. As a result, Taiwan, a nation of 21 million people,[3] has accumulated currency reserves of 98.7 billion dollars,[4] the second largest in the world after Japan. South Korea, also, was creative in its use of both tariff and non-tariff barriers in its strategy for industrialization. To avoid domestic prices getting too far out of line, the government from time to time authorized certain imports. This prevented windfall profits and maintained pressure on local industry, encouraging it to continue to seek export markets.

As Cheryl Payer explains in *Lent and Lost: Foreign Credit and Third World Development*,[5] the first point to remember, when the Western institutions explain their version of the reasons for Asia's economic miracle, is that its fundamental lesson is not to allow foreign sellers to invade your domestic market.

Professor Kay is wrong again when he suggests that, historically, the nations which have grown richer most quickly are those which opened their markets to liberalized trade. During the nineteenth century, when its growth surpassed that of Great Britain and it became the world's dominant economic force, the United States was systematically protectionist.[6] Profoundly influenced by Alexander Hamilton, its first Secretary of the Treasury (1789–95), and his book *Report on Manufactures* (1791), the US pursued a policy of strict protectionism from 1816 to 1846. In that year restrictions were relaxed to a more moderate level, until in 1861 the government reverted to a firmer policy.[7]

Between 1870 and 1892, the US increased the protection of its home market at a time of very rapid economic growth. Continental Europe, on the other hand, which had adopted a policy of relatively free trade between 1860 and 1879, was gripped by a great depression.[8] In the years following 1875, the US applied a tariff on manufactured goods in the range of 40 per cent to 50 per cent. In Continental Europe, tariffs were between 9 per cent and 12 per cent.[9] American industry, protected from competing European products, was able to focus on imports of products necessary in establishing its industrial infrastructure and, therefore, its future manufacturing might.[10]

More recently, the economic miracle that took place in Japan during the 1950s and 1960s was nourished by a system of formal and indirect protectionism. The GATT agreement of 1994 is intended to remove much of this protection, and the impact on Japan could be substantial.

In Continental Europe, the period from 1945 to 1974 is generally described as 'the thirty glorious years' of economic growth. Here again, protectionism was in place. The European Economic Community's internal market encouraged free trade, but a common tariff was applied on imports from countries outside the Community. General de Gaulle never accepted the concept of global free trade and believed in Community preference. At his press conference on 14 January 1963, he stated: 'The question is whether Great Britain can now, along with the Continent, accept a truly common tariff . . .'[11]

Britain, the birthplace of the Industrial Revolution, was the exception. By the mid-nineteenth century, power in the country had shifted from the landowners and farming communities to the new industrial barons. The repeal of the Corn Laws in 1846 and the further liberalization of international trade provided British industry with everything it wanted: a flow of cheap labour driven from the land to the towns by the effects of imported agricultural products, cheap imported food to feed them, a flow of funds to the colonies in payment for their exports of commodities, and a return of those funds to Britain to buy manufactured goods. Britain's dominant industrial position ensured that the exported funds returned home. That, of course, has changed dramatically. All that now remains is the unchallenged, outdated, conventional wisdom that emerged from circumstances which prevailed uniquely in Britain during the nineteenth century.

There is a widely-held belief that the 1929 crash and the Great Depression were triggered by the Smoot–Hawley Tariff Act, which increased tariffs on imports into the US.[12] Professor Murray Weidenbaum's statement quoted at the beginning of this chapter is typical. Vice-President Al Gore used Smoot–Hawley as a reference point on two occasions during the Gore–Perot debate on NAFTA in November 1993:

> This is a picture of Mr Smoot and Mr Hawley. They look like pretty good fellas. They sounded reasonable at the time. A lot of people believed them . . . They raised tariffs, and it was one of the principal causes – many economists say the principal cause – of the Great Depression in this country and around the world.[13]

In fact, the Smoot–Hawley Tariff Act was not passed into law until 17 June 1930, whereas the stock market crashed in October 1929. In 1929, the unemployment rate was estimated to be 3.2 per cent. It rose sharply throughout 1930 to reach 8.7 per cent by the end of that year, before the effect of the tariffs could reasonably have been felt by industry.[14]

In 1929, imports represented about 4.2 per cent[15] of the GNP of the US, amounting to about 4.3 billion dollars.[16] Smoot–Hawley raised the average tariff on all goods from 14.5 to 15.9 per cent. The Act altered

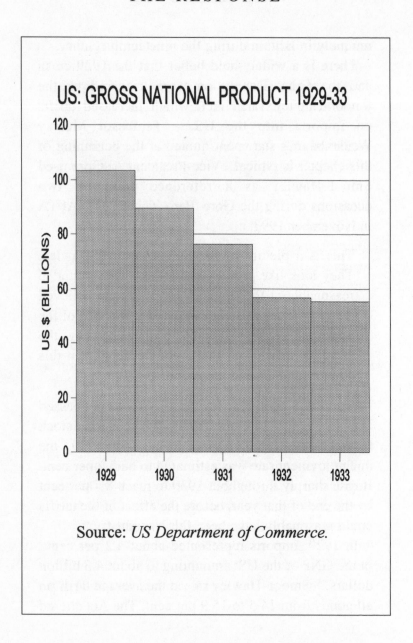

US: GROSS NATIONAL PRODUCT 1929-33

Source: *US Department of Commerce.*

tariffs on only one-third of US imports, i.e. on imports to a value of about 1.4 billion dollars in 1929. During 1930 the gross amount of imports of dutiable products declined by 462 million dollars. As Smoot–Hawley was enacted in June 1930, it is estimated that the total impact of the Tariff Act in 1930 was limited to the amount of increased duty on only 231 million dollars of imports, a negligible figure.[17]

It is important to note that the volume of duty-free imports dropped by similar proportions to that of products on which duty had been raised by Smoot–Hawley. For example, in 1930 and 1931, duty-free imports dropped by 29 per cent and 52 per cent respectively, whereas imports of products affected by Smoot–Hawley dropped by 27 per cent and 51 per cent.[18] This very small amount of protection, we are asked to believe, caused a 46 per cent drop in the GNP of the US, from 103.4 billion dollars in 1929 to 55.4 billion dollars in 1933 (see chart on opposite page).[19]

The true cause of the 1929 crash and subsequent depression was the breakdown of a grotesquely overheated financial system. In fact, the economy was still growing strongly when the crash occurred. Industrial production in November 1929 was 7 per cent higher than in November 1928, and started to fall in January 1930,[20] months before Smoot–Hawley became law.

THE RESPONSE

Senator John Heinz (R–Pa), speaking in the Senate on 9 May 1983, said:

> Every time someone in the administration or the Congress gives a speech about a more aggressive trade policy . . ., others, often in the academic community or in the Congress, immediately react with speeches on the return of Smoot–Hawley, and the dark days of blatant protectionism.
>
> A return to Smoot–Hawley, of course, is intended to mean a return to depression, unemployment, poverty, misery and even war . . . Now, however, someone has dared to explode this myth publicly through an economic analysis of the actual tariff increases in the Act and their effects in the early years of the depression . . . Mr President, I ask that the study, by Don Bedell of Bedell Associates, be printed into the Record.[21]

The conclusion of the Bedell Associates report is that 'No basis exists for any claim that Smoot–Hawley had a distinctively devastating effect on imports beyond and separate from the impact of the economic collapse in 1929.'[22] During the early 1930s, twenty-five countries increased their import duties.[23] But by then the world was in a global crisis, and these protectionist measures were the consequence of the financial collapse and not a cause of it.

THE RESPONSE

I have already reminded readers that the economic emergence of America, post-war Germany, the nations that formed the European Economic Community, Japan and the newly industrialized countries took place within systems of protectionism. However, protectionism could have a cost, as Paul Goodman writes, in the case of a small industrialized market which cuts itself off from the world and protects its industry while also allowing corporatism or socialism to dominate its economy.

My proposal is wholly different. It is merely that Europe should respect the principle of Community preference. This means that the internal European market would be based on the free movement of goods and capital and would be subject to the general rules that are a prerequisite of free enterprise. Europe and NAFTA are the largest marketplaces that have ever come about. To suggest that the European Union is not, already, large enough to allow effective competition within its borders is equivalent to suggesting that competition could never have existed at any time anywhere in the world. Europe consists of fifteen nations with a population of 370 million people and a combined GDP in 1994 of 7,313 billion dollars, compared with NAFTA's 7,571 billion dollars.[24]

Bilateral trading agreements could be entered into with other regions of the world as long as they are beneficial to the fundamental interests of the national economy and not just of the corporate economy. My belief is that if a foreign company wishes to sell its products in Europe it should invest in Europe, and we should welcome that investment. Foreign companies would bring to Europe their capital and their technology, build factories in Europe, employ Europeans and truly contribute to the European economy. As long as the rules are in place to avoid cartels, price-fixing and other anticompetitive structures, Europe would be a vast, open and free market which would welcome innovations from anywhere in the world.

European companies wishing to invest in NAFTA or Latin America would behave in a like fashion, participating directly in the regional economy and playing their part in the enhancement of national prosperity.

Turning now to the comments of Norman Macrae, it is disappointing that a former Deputy Editor of the *Economist* seems unable to identify the difference between a regional economy based on free enterprise and another which was controlled by a communist, totalitarian system. Recently we have witnessed the effects of protectionism within a contemporary context. Alan Tonelson, Research Director of the Economic Strategy Institute of Washington DC, published a study[25] analysing five American industries which received 'significant relief from imports through intelligently structured trade laws' –

in other words, protection. His conclusion is that 'those industries have confounded the predictions of laissez-faire economic ideologies by gaining market share at home and in some cases abroad, contributing to job creation and reinvigorating American competitiveness':

> The notion that import relief can achieve lasting net benefits clashes violently with the prevailing wisdom of laissez-faire economics. Protectionism of any kind or degree, many economists insist, only shelters inefficient companies . . . In particular, this orthodoxy teaches that industries and companies receiving import relief grow lazy and greedy. Shielded from competition, these firms allegedly lose incentives to innovate, boost efficiency and hold down prices. Instead, they rest on their technological laurels, forget about quality, jack up prices and greedily suck windfall profits out of captive markets.

> These textbook staples . . . have been completely contradicted by much of America's recent experience with import relief. The US automobile, semiconductor, machine tool, steel and textile industries all received significant import relief throughout the 1980s and 1990s. In all five industries – which total hundreds of

companies, employ millions of workers and span the technological spectrum – new investments in plant, equipment and research and development surged, productivity shot up, quality improved and prices rose at rates very close to overall inflation rates, and sometimes below them.

I have included more details from Alan Tonelson's report in Appendix B to this chapter.

APPENDIX A

Protectionism and the economic rise of Taiwan and Korea

The *Far East Economic Review* wrote in 1988 that 'Throughout [Taiwan's post-war development] the Taiwan government has played an enormous role in the economy – controlling [it] through a combination of direct investment in strategic industries and regulation of exchange rates, business licences, import duties and trade restrictions.'[1]

On 4 July 1983, the US *de facto* representative to Taiwan, in an interview with the *Economic News,* explained:

> US exports to Taiwan face a number of significant trade barriers, ranging from the indirect, such as excessive customs duties, to outright import bans . . . Many items, covering the spectrum from general household goods to kitchenware to processed and packaged foods and even to orange juice concentrate, have as much as 70 per cent added to their cost before they reach the market . . . Word-processing equipment has duties

as high as 30 per cent . . . Kraft liner board and packing materials may be assessed as high as 44 per cent . . . Last year, an import ban was placed on basic industrial-use petrochemicals such as PVC, LDPE and HDPE in order to protect producers. It transpired that domestic producers were not able to meet market demand and petrochemicals were imported under an 'orderly marketing' scheme . . . Imports of frozen poultry, pears and peanuts are banned . . . just recently the Council for Agricultural Planning and Development prepared a list of 148 agricultural products for which it wants to restrict imports or raise custom duties. Local content regulations requiring domestically produced parts to be used in manufacturing and mandatory exports for foreign investors are further barriers to free trade. We see this occurring now in the electronics industry . . . There are problems with health and safety standards for US pharmaceutical and health products because the Taiwan authorities do not consider US Food and Drug Administration certifications to be sufficient evidence of safety, even though they are accepted in most other parts of the world. US service industries, such as accounting, insurance and shipping, face restrictions here that do not apply to their Taiwan counterparts operating in the United States . . . "[2]

THE RESPONSE

Between 1956 and 1966, the share of items covered by import control, including those categorized as 'prohibited', varied from 46 per cent to 41 per cent. Meanwhile, tariff rates on about half all dutiable products were in the range of 41.4 per cent to 58.5 per cent.[3]

Non-tariff barriers, many of which were used by Taiwan, include quantitative restrictions, such as quotas; limitations on the source of procurement or on the qualifications of import applicants; a requirement for documents of approval from domestic competitors; multiple regulations including health, sanitary, quality standards, domestic content requirements and supplementary import charges. For example, imports of most steel items until 1987 had to be approved by China Steel, Taiwan's large steel producing company.[4]

A study by Tu and Wang[5] showed that over half of imports in 1984, based on their value, were restricted in various ways. For example, 29 per cent needed approval from a domestic agency or ministry and 21 per cent were limited by the status of those who were entitled to import them. K.Y. Yin, the principal architect of Taiwan's economic strategy, explained that 'in the enforcement of the policy of protection, tariff and the control of imports are methods which should be used at the same time. A protection tariff itself lacks flexibility and cannot fully attain the objective of protection. The control of imports is more flexible in its operation because it can be readjusted from time to time in accordance with the actual requirement.'[6]

At the same time as Taiwan protected its domestic market, it aggressively encouraged exports. Exporters received rebates on tariffs paid on imported products destined to be used in subsequent exports. Exporters were not always allowed to import products where domestically-produced alternatives were available. They were only permitted to import 'controlled' items if the price of the domestic equivalent was at least 10 per cent higher than that of the imported product.[7] But 'if they give enough reason, if they have a special case, they can import a restricted item.'[8] Exporters benefited from special tax incentives, export credits, government-assisted export promotion and special export processing zones.

Like Taiwan, South Korea protected its home market in a flexible way and actively promoted exports. A study by the Development Centre of the Organization for Economic Cooperation and Development[9] shows that the rapid industrialization of South Korea has to a large extent been achieved through 'import controls' effected by 'high import duties'. 'Given these protectionist measures,' remarks the author, mining output and manufacturing output have grown by 15 per cent annually between 1953 and 1960. The policy was followed throughout the 1960s and 1970s, when 'increases in import duties except on essential goods, restrictions on international borrowing and an emphasis on the growth of exports' were employed. Imports of restricted items were allowed when they were in the national interest,[10] but by 1968 average legal tariffs had reached 54 per cent. They were accompanied by a complex system of quantitative restrictions.[11]

Other studies of the late 1960s and early 1970s indicate effective rates of protection of 67 per cent for consumer durables and 106 per cent for transport.[12] In 1978 and 1982, the effective rate of protection for manufactured products averaged 49 per cent.[13] In 1978, during a strongly protectionist phase, imports classified as restricted accounted for 75 per cent by value of all manufactured imports.[14]

APPENDIX B

A *study of the practical effects of the protectionist agreements negotiated by the Reagan Administration*

In 1981, the Reagan Administration secured protection for the automobile industry. Alan Tonelson writes:[1] 'By 1985, investment in new plant and equipment had reached a level double that of 1975 in real terms. And despite the explosion of technology-intensive information industries during the 1980s, the automobile industry slightly increased its share of total US corporate research and development spending, to 12.4 per cent. By 1984, the Big Three [General Motors, Ford and Chrysler]'s productivity was rising at a 6.5 per cent annual rate, compared with 3.3 per cent for all US manufacturing.'

In addition, after protection was introduced, 'the prices of American-made passenger cars increased less . . . than before'. And the Big Three increased their share of the US market.

'Starting in the 1970s, the US steel industry went into a tailspin . . . America's share of world steel production fell from over 50 per cent at the end of World War Two to 26 per cent in 1960 and 14.2 per cent in 1980 . . . Foreign steel sales rose from 12.4 per cent of the US market in 1973 . . . to a peak of 26.4 per cent in 1984 . . . [The] United States has been the only major industrialized country to be a consistent net importer of steel in recent years.'

In 1984, the Reagan Administration negotiated a number of bilateral, protectionist trade agreements which went into effect in 1987. They limited imports of finished steel to 18.5 per cent of the US market and imports of semifinished steel products to 20.2 per cent of the market. 'Whereas the steel industry's capital expenditures fell from 2.6 billion dollars in 1980 to 862 million dollars in 1986, purchases of new plant and equipment bounced back to 2.5 billion dollars by 1990.'

Additionally, Japanese and South Korean companies, seeking access to the North American markets, invested 3 billion dollars in cutting-edge technology in American facilities. The increase in capital investment and high-technology mini-mills greatly improved productivity, and a cheaper dollar 'enabled US companies – led by the mini-mills – to become among the world's lowest-cost steel producers'.

In 1986, foreign machine-tool makers held 62 per cent of the US market. That year, the Reagan Administration negotiated protective trade agreements with Japan and Taiwan. 'The ratio of capital spending to depreciation soared from 80 cents on the dollar to 1.61 dollars spent on new equipment for every dollar taken in depreciation.' Research and development spending jumped from 5.2 per cent of sales in 1987 to 11.9 per cent in 1992. Prices charged by protected firms rose only slightly. From 1986 to 1992, machine-tool exports doubled to 1 billion dollars and import penetration in the US market dropped from its 1986 peak of 62 per cent to 49 per cent.

The world market share of US - based chipmakers fell from 57 per cent in 1981 to 40 per cent in 1987. 'In both 1985 and 1986, the US industry reported losses of nearly 2 billion dollars and 25,000 workers lost good jobs at good wages.' In 1986, the Reagan Administration negotiated protection from Japan and then, in 1987, imposed punitive tariffs on many Japanese imports. 'The American semiconductor industry accelerated its retooling efforts. Research and development expenditures continued to increase at a whopping 17 per cent annual rate . . . Labour productivity soared at an impressive 16 per cent annual rate . . . US producers introduced scores of innovative products to world markets. And producer prices . . . increased only 4 per cent between 1982 and 1991.' By 1992, US-based companies had 'moved into a tie with their Japan-based competitors in the world'.

THE RESPONSE

Since the late 1950s, the textile and apparel industries have been partially protected. Since 1974, world trade in these products has been governed by the Multi-Fibre Arrangement, which under GATT will be phased out over ten years. During the last decade, 'annual new capital expenditures for textile mill products have climbed, in real terms, from 1.6 billion dollars in 1980 to 2.5 billion dollars in 1993.' Productivity has increased by more than 77 per cent between 1980 and 1992. Producer prices for textiles, since 1982, have risen by less than the figure for all industrial commodities.

'Import relief measures helped convince industries that they were not stuck with trying to buck impossible odds . . . Import relief programmes signalled to executives that their industries could indeed have a future . . .'.

3

Global free trade and its effects on jobs and wages in developed economies.

The European Commission, document of 18 October 1994:

'There is no evidence that foreign competition is a major cause of either [unemployment or reduced wages in the industrialized economies] . . . In the case of France, there is no evidence that openness to trade has generated substantial unemployment . . . To summarize: trade with low wage economies does not cause major reductions in total employment or real earnings . . .'

'Competition from low-wage countries does not cause generally lower wages in industrialized countries. The development is rather the other way around, with wages increasing in rapidly developing countries in line with productivity.'

'The main causes of unemployment are to be found in technological developments.'

Brian Hindley, 'The Goldsmith Fallacy':

'Nor does a glance at the statistics of trade suggest that trade with developing countries has caused, or could have caused, significant unemployment in the European Union.'

'There are a number of careful empirical studies of the impact of different factors on employment in high-wage areas. They typically conclude that the effect of trade is small relative to that of technological change.'

'A flood of new entrants into world labour markets puts at risk the employment of persons in high-wage areas . . . and who currently earn their living from activities that can be performed as well in low-wage areas . . . If such persons cannot acquire more valuable skills or find employment in occupations not threatened by international trade, the wages they will be able to obtain may be very low – so low that they may prefer to remain unemployed.'

'But the counterpart of low wages is low productivity . . . The general level of wages is lower in developing countries than in the European Union because productivity in general is lower in developing countries than in the European Union.'

'Sir James seems concerned . . . that all goods can be produced more cheaply in low-wage countries than in high-wage countries . . . Such a situation is conceivable. But if prices and exchange rates are such that all potential purchases are in one direction, a massive maladjustment in the macro-economic relations between economies is implied: local currency, wage and price levels are wrong . . . But if the European Union or its member states were to find themselves in such a situation, the sensible solution would be to adjust the macro-economic relationships, not to block trade.'

John Kay, Daily Telegraph, *28 December 1994:*

'The reason wages are so low in the Philippines and Vietnam is that labour there is not, in the main, very productive.'

THE RESPONSE

The year 1974 marked a turning point in Europe. The 'thirty glorious years' of growth in the European Economic Community gave way to a period in which economic growth has been accompanied by massively rising unemployment.

Maurice Allais, France's only Nobel Prize laureate for economics, points out that the years since 1974 have been dominated by the perverse effects of global free trade and the distortions of the international monetary system.[1] In France, despite an 80 per cent expansion in GNP, underemployment between 1974 and 1993 grew by an average of 210,000 people each year to reach a level of 18.6 per cent of the active population (see Chart 9, page 139).[2] Allais uses the term 'underemployed' because, since 1973, programmes to take people off the register of unemployed have caused the official unemployment figures to drop without creating new jobs.

It is now recognized worldwide that the widely used International Labour Organization definition of unemployment fails to reflect all elements of labour market slack. In a recent report, the Organization for Economic Cooperation and Development estimated that there were some 15 million 'involuntary part-time workers' and another 4 million 'discouraged workers' in addition to the 34 million people who meet the ILO unemployment criteria in the OECD countries.[3] Other reports such as that by the United Kingdom's Royal Statistical Society,[4] or by the US government's Bureau of Labor Statistics,[5] have also considered the changing patterns of work in the global marketplace and the shortcomings of the standard ILO unemployment measure. Charts of unemployment and underemployment in the UK, France and the European Community (where figures exist) will be found on pages 133, 139 and 141.

Allais goes on to explain that the massive rise in unemployment in France cannot be the result of specifically French conditions because, using the standard definition of the International Labour Organization, French unemployment and that of the European Community are as a whole very similar. He concludes that the shared trend can only be explained by factors that are common to both France and the European Community.[6]

Furthermore, Allais observes that 'this underlying trend is not a worldwide phenomenon. And it cannot be attributed to technological progress, because, during the same period of time, the unemployment rate in Japan only rose from 1.3 per cent to 2.2 per cent . . . From 1974 to 1991, industrial employment in the EEC dropped by 15.4 per cent, whereas in Japan it rose by 13.2 per cent.'[7] Throughout this period, Japan was a world leader in applying cutting-edge technology to its industrial production. And Japan also maintained her system of protectionism.

Whereas Europe has sought to protect the level of wages, the US has aimed to protect employment by adopting a policy of 'flexibility', meaning that wages should be allowed to fall so as to reflect the conditions of the marketplace. With the creation of a global market for labour, since 1973 the weekly and hourly earnings of US production and non-supervisory workers (80 per cent of the US workforce) have fallen in real terms by 19.2 per cent and 13.4 per cent respectively (see Chart 12, page 145).[8] Nonetheless, as the Economic Policy Institute and Dr Herman Starobin have argued, the official US figures understate the true position of unemployment.[9]

Remarkably, after affirming repeatedly that global trade does not affect employment, Hindley states:

> A flood of new entrants into world labour markets puts at risk the employment of persons in high-wage areas . . . and who currently earn their living from activities that can be performed as well in low-wage areas. If such persons cannot acquire more valuable skills or find employment in occupations not threatened by international trade, the wages they will be able to obtain may be very low – so low that they may prefer to remain unemployed.

This statement clearly accepts that competition from low-wage areas threatens both jobs and levels of pay. And it demonstrates a naive belief that the welfare state will be perpetuated regardless of the state of the economy and that those who prefer to remain unemployed will continue to be paid.

Turning to the question of productivity, recent experience in both a developed and a developing economy demonstrates that, in reality, wages do not increase 'in line with productivity'. Since 1973, productivity in the US has risen by 23.2 per cent.[10] As we have seen, during the same period real weekly and hourly wages have dropped by 19.2 per cent and 13.4 per cent.[11] Meanwhile in Mexico, between 1980 and 1992 productivity rose by 48 per cent while salaries (adjusted for inflation) fell by 21 per cent.[12]

Only in economies which are protected and in which there is reasonably full employment can wages rise more or less in line with productivity. But in a world economy based on global free trade, the labour market necessarily becomes a global market, with a virtually limitless reservoir of unemployed labour. According to the International Labour Organization, some 30 per cent of the world's workforce, about 820 million people, are either unemployed or underemployed.[13] The companies which dominate world trade – the transnational corporations – are footloose. They will move production wherever labour is cheapest. As the International Labour Organization explains: 'Location decisions nowadays are very finely tuned to labour costs,'[14] and as cutting-edge technology and capital can be transferred instantaneously anywhere in the world, factories can be located anywhere. With vast numbers of able and trainable people seeking employment at any price, the level of wages will be determined not by productivity but by the old-fashioned measure of supply and demand.

Newsweek describes the phenomenon graphically. Typically a multinational corporation now is a:

> down-sized, out-sourced and largely stateless web of cross-border corporate alliances . . . In the last decade the world's 37,000 multinational or transnational companies . . . have been responsible for more in sales than all the world's trade exports put together: 5.8 trillion dollars in 1992, the most recent year of reliable data. In the United States, which has by far the most multinationals, 80 per cent of the dollar goods sold abroad are not exported but sold under governance of multinationals, either sales by affiliates, intrafirm trade, or through licensing or franchising agreements.[15]

This means that despite the commercial success in world markets of US-based transnationals, a large part of the products they sell is manufactured not in the US but, increasingly, in low-cost regions. The effect of selling these products at home and internationally under US labels has, of course, been to increase imports and decrease exports. Chart 13 on page 147 illustrates the rise in the US trade deficit following the implementation of GATT.

There is a difference between today's transnational companies and the old multinationals. Multinationals built factories in Brazil or India in order to conquer the Brazilian or Indian markets, not in order to acquire cheap labour to replace jobs at home. They participated productively in the economies of the countries in which they invested and did so without damaging their own national economies. Transnationals, on the other hand, buy labour in low-wage countries and import their products for sale in the residual high-wage, high-income markets. Today many of the larger groups have become hybrids. When Sony manufactures televisions in France for sale in the European Union, it is acting as a multinational. When it imports, for sale in Europe, televisions produced in low-wage areas, it is acting as a transnational.

Thus, a transnational company, behaving in this way, creates unemployment in its home base and increases its nation's trade deficit.

Hindley's most remarkable statement, also quoted at the beginning of this chapter, is:

> Sir James seems concerned . . . that all goods can be produced more cheaply in low-wage countries than in high-wage countries . . . But if prices and exchange rates are such that all potential

61

purchases are in one direction, a massive maladjustment in the macro-economic relations between economies is implied: local currency, wage and price levels are wrong . . . But if the European Union or its member states were to find themselves in such a situation, the sensible solution would be to adjust the macro-economic relationships, not to block trade.

By adjusting the 'macro-economic relationships' Hindley means adjusting 'local currency, wage and price levels'. He is suggesting that if too many goods from low-wage countries are purchased we must reduce total earnings, either directly or through devaluing our currency, to a level which would allow us to compete with low-wage countries. A glance at Chart 8 on page 137 will indicate the potential pain of pursuing such a policy.

Hindley would prefer to reduce earnings substantially rather than 'block trade'. In other words, he would prefer to sacrifice the well-being of the nation rather than his free-trade ideology.

He has forgotten that the purpose of the economy is to serve society, not the other way round. A successful economy increases wages, employment and social stability. Reducing wages is a sign of failure. There is no glory in competing in a worldwide race to lower the standard of living of one's own nation.

APPENDIX

Reports and anecdotes about the transfer of production and services to low-wage countries

On 27 August 1995 the *New York Times* wrote:

> Texas Instruments Inc. is designing some of its more sophisticated computer chips in India. Motorola Inc. recently set up computer-programming and equipment design centres in China, India, Singapore, Hong Kong, Taiwan and Australia, and it is looking for a site in South America. While big American banks already process some account statements overseas, large accounting firms and insurance companies are looking at ways to prepare tax returns and handle insurance claims in East Asia.
>
> . . . [The] combination of powerful personal computers and high-capacity undersea telephone cables is also subjecting millions of white-collar Americans to the same global wage pressures that their blue-collar counterparts have long struggled with . . .

THE RESPONSE

Many fear that the growing tendency of corporations to farm out tasks to developing countries is widening the gap even further between the rich and everybody else in American society by eliminating some categories of high-skill, high-wage jobs that make up the heart of the middle class. But the temptation to use cheap foreign labour is too great for companies that are desperate to stay competitive in an increasingly global marketplace.[1]

In February 1995, the Economic Research Department of the AFL–CIO published an analysis of the 'Expanding Influence in the 1990s of Multinational Corporations'.[2] Here are a few of their conclusions:

– 'With US markets absorbing one-half of all manufactured goods produced in developing countries, the trade surpluses enjoyed by these countries directly contribute to trade deficits in the United States and ultimately cost American workers their jobs.'

– In 1992, of total imports into the United States, '41 per cent (216 billion dollars) was shipped and/or received by multinationals. About 109 billion dollars, or more than 20 per cent, of all US merchandise imports are directly attributable to the foreign affiliates of US companies. Nearly all of these imports were shipped direct to the parent company in the United States. Some 107 billion dollars was received by US multinational corporations from other foreign sources.'

– Turning to exports, the report indicates: 'More than 120 billion dollars' worth of merchandise exports were shipped to foreign affiliates of US multinational corporations . . . Much of this represents outlays for plants and equipment in foreign production operations that ship their products back to the US for sale.'

– 'The countries with the fastest growth in jobs attributed to US multinationals are China, Costa Rica and Mexico.'

– VTech Holdings Ltd, a Hong Kong company 'with a 70 per cent share of the US market for computer-based educational toys' and which 'also produces cellular phones in a joint venture with Nokia Group and is a top supplier of high-end products to AT&T, Alcatel and Philips' employs between 11,000 and 13,000 people in China.

– 'The McDonnell Douglas MD-82 commercial transports are presently being manufactured . . . in Shanghai. Five of these Chinese-built aircraft have been sold to TWA and are now flying domestic US routes. . . . Meanwhile, Boeing . . . jointly produces many of the parts for its 737 with Chinese companies, including vertical and horizontal tails, fuselages, cargo doors and horizontal stabilizers. In addition, some of the parts for the 747 are now made in China, and a significant proportion of the all-new 777 will be produced there.'

– 'The transfer of valuable technology also presents serious future implications.'

According to Washington-based MBG Information Services, 'US industry losses to the so-called big emerging markets (BEMs)[3] . . . are far worse than ever before . . . The Department of Commerce announced this week that the 1995 US deficit with the BEMs is 47 per cent worse than 1994.' MBG estimate that losses will top 55 billion dollars in 1995.[4]

Hans-Olaf Henkel, president of the Federation of German Industries (BDI), writes in the *Wall Street Journal Europe*, 25 July 1995: 'The financial and social burden of our high unemployment has become unacceptable and unaffordable. More important, relocating production abroad is not a real solution for the majority of our Mittelstand.'[5] 'Mittelstand is the term used to describe Germany's small and medium-sized companies, often considered the backbone of Germany's economy. They are embedded in local communities, often managed by families, and therefore not structured for transnationalism. What is more, many are suppliers to the major corporations which as they move offshore will increasingly obtain supplies and services from local companies.

Edith Holleman, Counsel for the US House of Representatives Committee on Science, Space and Technology, told a meeting of engineers: 'As international corporations move their facilities to cheaper locations, jobs in fields such as product design, process engineering and software development are moving with them.'[6]

G. Pascal Zachary writes in the *Wall Street Journal Europe*: 'Coveted design jobs, once the sole province of the Santa Clara, California, company's US offices, have come to Malaysia too. Intel recently asked 100 engineers in Penang to design future chips, brain work formerly done by Americans in Arizona. The story is similar at Hewlett-Packard whose Penang factory each day makes a million light emitting diodes . . . Even so, Malaysia . . . is vulnerable as multinationals constantly look for sources of cheaper labour – raising the spectre that some could abandon Malaysia for a place where people toil for less.'[7]

Tony Walker writes in the *Financial Times*: 'Mr

THE RESPONSE

Oh Chan Kun, president of the Yantai Hanta Leather Product Company, makes no secret of the . . . reasons for moving its production . . . to China. "Wages had become too high in Korea," he says. "We came to China and to Yantai to take advantage of the lower labour costs."[8]

Terence Roth, also in the *Wall Street Journal Europe,* writes:

In April 1993 Asea Brown Boveri Ltd, the Swiss–Swedish engineering group, closed down production of engine starters at its Heidelberg, Germany, plant. Three months later, the line was restarted at ABB EJF in Brno, the Czech Republic – at one-tenth the labour cost. The same thing happened to a German ABB welding plant, reborn in Gdansk, Poland, and to German and Swiss plants that once rolled out air-cooled generators . . . "Business is business," smiles the lanky Mr Maximenko. "Price plays an increasing role in competition . . ."

Dutch workers at a fluorescent lighting plant of Philips NV, the Netherlands-based electronics group, went on a two-day strike to protest management plans to transfer production to Poland, China and India . . . "The decision was to move more production to low-wage and low-cost production regions . . ." a Philips spokesman explains.[9]

THE RESPONSE

During 1993, the Finance Commission of the French Senate held hearings on the impact of transferring French manufacturing activities to low-wage areas.[10] Here are some examples of the evidence presented:

– A large number of well-known international and national branded products are now almost totally produced in low-wage areas (for example, Lacoste, Benetton, Nike, Reebok, Adidas, Chaussures André).

– The chairman of Adidas testified that moving production to low-cost countries was inevitable for the survival of the company.

– Employment in France in the textile and apparel industries has dropped from 680,000 in 1975 to 347,000 in 1991, and to 282,000 in 1994.[11]

– The shoe industry has largely moved abroad. Employment in France has dropped from 70,000 in 1975 to 34,500 in 1992, and to 31,000 in 1994.[12]

– Employment in France in the clock and watch industry has fallen from 14,467 people in 1979 to 7,200 in 1992, and to 6,600 in 1994.[13]

THE RESPONSE

– 70 per cent of all toys in France are imported from South-East Asia.

– The electronics industry has moved a major part of its production to South-East Asia. In 1978 the industry employed 21,273 people in France. By 1991 this had fallen to 13,440; it now stands at 12,108.[14]

– France's largest consumer electronics company, Thomson Consumer Electronics, employs 18,200 people in Asia, amounting to 34 per cent of its workforce. Its sales in Asia represent only 3 per cent of its world sales; the remainder is shipped to other markets. The chairman of Thomson testified: 'With the current state of world competition, it is out of the question to manufacture elsewhere. If Europe moves to protect itself, it will be quite different. Technically we could repatriate production within twelve to eighteen months.'

– Asian imports of consumer electronics account for 41 per cent of the French domestic market. This understates the true position. A large number of products which are assembled in France and are described as being French use numerous parts imported from Asia.

– The Finance Commission estimated that of a total of 300,000 jobs now available for computer scientists, 50,000 to 80,000 could be moved abroad in the years ahead.

After reviewing the evidence the Commission stated: 'It seems reasonable to estimate that at least 3 to 5 million further jobs are directly threatened by the transfer of production to low-wage areas.' Yet the European Commission continues to assert that there is no evidence that foreign competition is a major cause of either unemployment or reduced wages in the industrialized economies.

4

Why financial outflows
resulting from trade
deficits of developed
countries will not
necessarily be recycled
indefinitely.

The European Commission, document of 19 October 1994:

'Outflows will over time match inflows. If the countries of Asia export more than they import, the excess cash will be invested abroad and ultimately the inflow will equal the outflow suffered by those with a trade deficit.'

Norman Macrae, Sunday Times, *12 December 1994:*[1]

'Suppose (in fun, not realism) that . . . all present world-tradable manufactures and services fled to [low-wage countries]. . . [They] could then do three things with their export surplus . . . Either (a) hoard it in foreign exchange; or (b) use it to buy everybody's ICIs and other principal industries; or (c) buy new goods and services from the West.

   Course (a) . . . would be loveliest for us. [The low-wage countries] would put all their hugely expanded export earnings in American and British and other foreign bonds . . . We could then import their nice cheap goods (much reducing our cost of living) at near-nil net foreign exchange drain, and expand our budget deficits . . . to create internal jobs and live the life of Riley.'

Paul Goodman, Sunday Telegraph, *6 November 1994:*

'So, if the developing nations develop vast trade surpluses, they will have to invest the proceeds somewhere – and, in due course, these will flow back to cover the trade deficits of Western nations.'

THE RESPONSE

The idea that accounts must balance, and that inflows must ultimately match outflows, is an accountant's idea.

But there is a fundamental misunderstanding here. If you make a loss, perhaps because you own a business that is trading unprofitably or because you have made a bad investment, you will not get rid of the loss by borrowing the amount needed to pay for it. You will have avoided or postponed a personal liquidity crisis, but you will still be poorer by the amount of the loss. You will also have to pay interest on the loan.

Alternatively, you might sell your house and rent somewhere else to live. You will have used the proceeds of the sale to pay your debts, but you will remain poorer by the value of the house. And in future, you will have to pay rent.

When the Asian countries, as mentioned by the European Commission, invest their 'excess cash' abroad, normally they do so by buying into businesses or by lending money. The latter normally takes the form either of buying government debt or of deposits, say in sterling or dollars, in the banking system. Now consider the position of the nations which, unlike the Asian countries, import more than they export and which, as a result, have a deficit as opposed to an excess of cash.

To finance their deficit, businesses or other assets are sold and debt is issued. This puts them in exactly the same position as an individual who sells his house or borrows money to cover his debts. Such a haemorrhage can last only a limited time before ending in bankruptcy.

America is just beginning to understand this. In its issue of 5 November 1994, the *Economist* stated: 'Since 1981, America has shifted from being the world's biggest creditor to its biggest debtor, thanks to its persistent current account deficits.'[1] An editorial in the *Washington Post* dated 3 November 1994 stated:

> Note that the American economy is now borrowing abroad to pay interest on its earlier foreign borrowings. That is no healthier for a country than it is for a business or a household. And how long can it go on? As long as foreigners are willing to lend. If and when their willingness diminishes, you will see it in higher interest rates. Should that happen, Americans would, as the economists say, have to adjust. That, as the Latin American debtor countries can testify, means a lower standard of living. The longer the foreign deficits pile up, the harder that adjustment will be.[2]

A nation's ability to borrow will depend on its credit-worthiness, as it does for an individual. And the credit-worthiness of the West is extremely doubtful. The table opposite shows the amounts already owed

COUNTRY DEBT AS A PERCENTAGE OF GDP

Country	Gross Debt*	Net pension liabilities¶	Total Debt
US†	64.6	66	130.6
Japan	78.7	218	296.7
Italy	123.2	233	356.2
Germany	53.2	160	213.2
France	56	216	272
Canada	95.6	250	345.6
UK	51.8	186	237.8
Belgium	142	165	307
G7‡	74.7	190	264.7

*Gross debt = gross financial commitments in 1994.
¶Net pension liabilities in 1990.
†US figure is for federal debt only.
‡Unweighted average for the G7 countries.

Source: Organization for Economic
Cooperation and Development.[3]

by European nations relative to their GDP. These figures are alarming, and they continue to rise as governments spend more than they receive. Most of these deficits are due to government expenditure aimed at softening the effects and even masking the existence of rapidly growing unemployment. In the *Wall Street Journal Europe*, Jean-Michel Paul points out that the average of the combined financial and pension debt of the G7 nations[4] as a percentage of GDP is above 260 per cent. Belgium and Italy are above 300 per cent.[5]

The case of Belgium is particularly illuminating. Its critical financial position has cast doubts on its future political stability. Belgium's political and business leaders see salvation in merging their country into a European suprastate, which would bail it out by effectively endorsing its debts. To achieve this, they desperately try to improve the appearance of the country's current financial situation.

So as to halt the rise in the national debt, they raise money by accelerating the programme of privatization. This produces non-recurring inflows of funds. They point to their balance-of-trade surplus, without mentioning that this is principally the result of a fall in consumption in the domestic market which itself reflects the very high real level of unemployment.[6] As Mr Paul writes in the *Wall Street Journal Europe*:

THE RESPONSE

It is increasingly clear that the policy response to the European debt crisis will include options that will significantly affect the contract between the borrower-state and the lenders. These options might take the form of policies such as default on debt and forced debt restructuring. Governments might also turn to monetary instruments with inflationary consequences.[7]

To put it simply, they might not repay you at all, or they might pay you in practically worthless devalued currency. This is not very good for future credit nor, therefore, for future borrowing.

The music stops when we are no longer considered credit-worthy. What would happen to Norman Macrae's scenario if the recycling of export surpluses were to cease, and those nations with trade surpluses and reserves only lent money to and invested in each other, as we in the developed world used to do? Macrae, at one time, almost recognized this risk. 1n 1993, he wrote of the 'emergence of some sort of Sino-Indian-Japanese currency bloc' and he warned Asian countries that the 'worst market errors' were made by governments which 'poured their official exchange reserves into dollars'.[8]

Furthermore, what particular goods and services would others seek to buy from the West? As America did in the nineteenth century, the newly emerging markets are increasingly buying equipment and technology with which to make their own industry and infrastructure even more competitive across an even broader range of activities. This category of imports is temporary, and represents no more than a transitional phase until the emerging countries can themselves produce products for their industrial infrastructure.

Far from the 'life of Riley', it is increasing unemployment and impoverishment that the West has to look forward to – unless it changes course, and in time.

5

Common markets between countries with widely differing wage rates and mutual poisoning. The results, so far, of NAFTA.

Tim Congdon, The Times, *18 November 1994:*

'But how can free trade be good and beneficial between Italy and Greece and between Mexico and the US but not between France and Turkey or Brazil and Canada?'

THE RESPONSE

Congdon's implication that I believe NAFTA is beneficial to its members is based on a misreading of my argument for regional free trade in *The Trap*. Never have I suggested that free trade is economically beneficial between countries with wholly different economies, and more particularly with widely varying wage rates.

However, other considerations can apply in the case of nations which share the same geographical area. Greece and Portugal are part of Europe and, therefore, we have good reasons for wishing to see them prosper. We might be able to help because they are small compared to the European Union as a whole. Out of a total EU population of 370 million, Greece has 10.4 million and Portugal has 9.8 million people;[1] their economies represent 1.1 per cent and 1.2 per cent of the EU's total GDP respectively.[2]

Creating a common market with Greece and Portugal is utterly different from trying to do the same with China or India. Even so, the process is very difficult and very costly. In *The Trap,* I outlined the problems faced by northern Italy in its attempt, over decades, to improve the economy of the less developed south.

Portugal used to be the country which supplied cheap labour to the European Union. It attracted substantial foreign capital seeking to invest in enterprises which manufacture products to sell in the high-wage markets of Europe. But after the fall of the Berlin Wall and the signing of the recent GATT agreements, Portuguese labour has become relatively expensive in comparison, for example, to that of Eastern Europe and Asia.

As a result, direct investment in Portugal plunged from a peak of 2.28 billion dollars in 1991 to 1.03 billion dollars in 1994.[3]   Emmanuel Figueredo, a Portuguese economist and co-author of a European Union report on foreign investment in Portugal, explains: 'in the long run, these companies [the transnational corporations] are extremely mobile, closing down and relocating when [host] countries lose their competitive edge.'[4]

The United States, Canada and Mexico also share a geographical identity. But Mexico's population has reached 93.7 million people and is growing fast.[5] Its culture, which is strong and deep-rooted, is very different from that of the US, as is its economy. The difference in wage rates alone is enormous, and the problems of integration will be huge.

On 10 December 1994, the *Economist* published an article which reflected the conventional wisdom of the conventional economists and their friends in government:

Listen carefully. Do you hear a giant sucking sound of jobs and investment disappearing from the United States across the Rio Grande to Mexico, as predicted by Ross Perot in the great argument over the North American Free Trade Agreement? A different noise is in the air: the hubbub of politicians singing the praises of trade liberalization.

It went on to quote Lloyd Bentsen, the departing Treasury Secretary, declaring that NAFTA was 'a win-win situation', with extra jobs on all sides. 'Boosters for the agreement,' added the *Economist,* 'are already explaining how it demonstrates that rich countries need not fear free trade with poor neighbours (West Europeans wary of opening their markets to the ex-communist East, please note).'[6]

On 20 December 1994, ten days after the *Economist* article appeared, reality forced itself onto the scene. The peso, which had been supported by incoming speculative money, collapsed. The Mexican economy followed, as did US exports to Mexico.

The overheating of the Mexican economy had been financed by too much short-term capital, partly in the form of short-term dollar-linked bonds known as 'Tesobonos' and partly in the form of portfolio investment from abroad, that is to say foreigners buying bonds and shares in Mexican companies. Portfolio investment is very volatile; unlike direct investment, it can come one day and leave the next (see chart opposite). Any loss of confidence can reverse the flow of funds and create a liquidity crisis. And so it was to be.

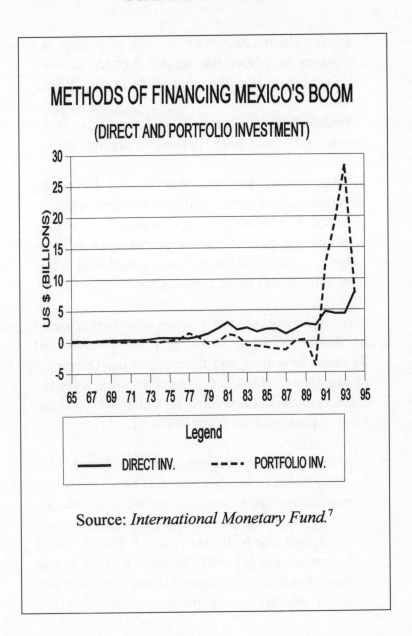

METHODS OF FINANCING MEXICO'S BOOM

(DIRECT AND PORTFOLIO INVESTMENT)

Legend

———— DIRECT INV.   - - - - PORTFOLIO INV.

Source: *International Monetary Fund.*[7]

Twenty months after NAFTA came into effect, we can begin to assess the results. Let us start by looking at them from the point of view of the United States.

Senator Byron L. Dorgan (D–ND), speaking in the Senate on 12 June 1995,[8] opened by saying:

> Some of us believed that if you linked an economy like ours, with an average wage of $15 to $17 an hour, to an economy like Mexico, which still pays in many areas 50 cents or $1 an hour . . . it would tip the table so that jobs in this country would move south to Mexico.

Senator Dorgan then referred to a new study released by Robert Scott of the Center for International Business Education and Research at the University of Maryland.[9] Scott had previously worked for the Joint Economic Committee in Congress. Senator Dorgan explained Scott's methods of analysis:

> Mr Scott takes out the transshipments between the two countries. In other words, if Mexico receives something that is actually produced in another nation – for example, computers from Asia – and re-exports them to the United States, those computers are not really Mexican exports and so they should not be counted in our measurement. Or if another nation produces something and

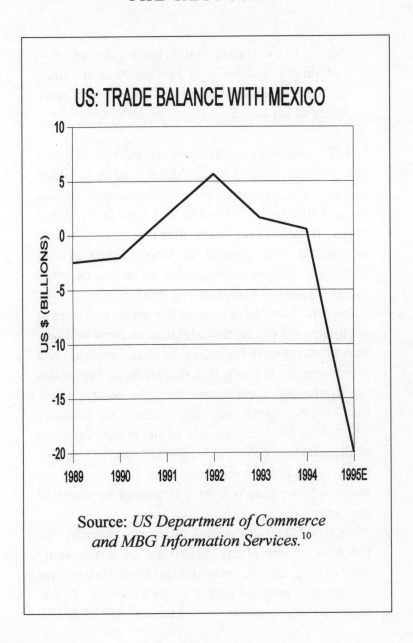

US: TRADE BALANCE WITH MEXICO

Source: *US Department of Commerce
and MBG Information Services.*[10]

ships it to the United States, but we do not use it and simply transfer it to Mexico, then it should not be considered an export from the United States to Mexico.[11]

In 1992, excluding transshipments, the United States had a trade surplus with Mexico of 5.7 billion dollars. US Department of Commerce figures suggest that in 1995 the US will have a 20 billion dollar trade deficit with Mexico. This would represent a swing against the United States of over 25 billion dollars, accompanied by a loss of about 220,000 jobs to Mexico during 1995.[12]

Imports from Mexico cover the whole spectrum of manufactured products. Mexican exports of high-tech products have boomed (see chart opposite) and recent reports indicate that the Mexican authorities are approving applications for two or three new maquiladora plants each day. These are factories situated on the Mexican side of the border designed to manufacture products for the US market. At this rate, in a little over one year the number of maquiladora plants will have increased by about 50 per cent.

As usual during a period of industrialization, the purchase of machinery necessary for establishing and extending the manufacturing infrastructure represents a growing part of overall imports. In due course, these imports into Mexico will diminish

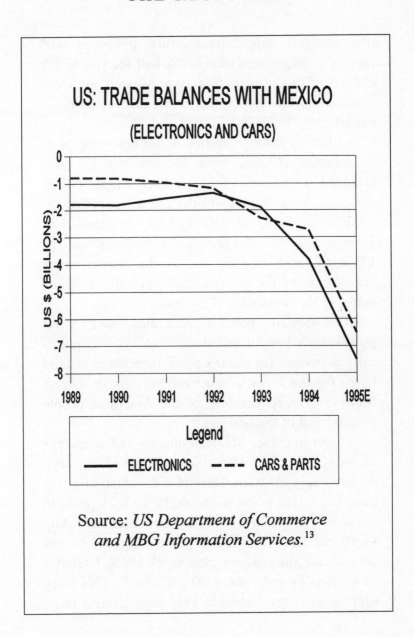

US: TRADE BALANCES WITH MEXICO
(ELECTRONICS AND CARS)

Source: *US Department of Commerce and MBG Information Services.*[13]

the products this infrastructure produces will increase. Supporters of NAFTA hail the rise in US exports of producer machinery to Mexico but avoid commenting on the evident consequences of those exports.

In addition to the 25 billion dollar deterioration in its balance of trade with Mexico, the US also arranged a 'bail-out' loan package of 50 billion dollars to Mexico to avoid the consequences of the liquidity crisis which followed the devaluation of December 1994. The principal contributor was the US itself, both directly and as the largest single contributor to the international institutions which made up the remainder of the loan.

From Mexico's point of view also, NAFTA has proven both painful and dangerous. It was politically necessary for the US administration to require terms for the loans which were very harsh indeed, because over 80 per cent of the American people disapproved of the bail-out.[14]

In order to reduce Mexican imports and encourage exports, the US effectively imposed a deep depression on Mexico. Despite a devaluation of the peso from 3.46 pesos to the dollar to 6.25 pesos to the dollar, and a rate of inflation now estimated at up to 50 per cent[15] (consumer prices surged 33.2 per cent during the first six months of 1995),[16] salaries have risen by only about 20 per cent.[17] This steep drop in earnings, linked to very high interest rates, was bound to produce a depression in the domestic market which would be partly offset by a steeply rising volume of exports. (Exports represented 25.3 per cent of total sales in the second quarter of 1995, compared to 10.3 per cent in same period in 1994).[18] Figures show that for the first half of 1995, the economy has contracted by 10 per cent.[19] During the great crisis of 1982–83, the fall in GNP amounted to only about 4 per cent. According to a survey conducted by the respected Center for Economic Studies of the Private Sector (CEESP), businesses in the three largest metropolitan areas of Mexico experienced an average sales decline of 23 per cent during the first half of 1995.[20]

As anticipated, the rise in exports and the fall in imports has resulted in an abrupt turnaround in Mexico's balance of trade, which in turn has stabilized, for the time being, the foreign exchange and securities markets. But the depression in Mexico has inevitably led to corporate bankruptcies, steeply rising unemployment and personal hardship.

As Mexicans come to Washington to testify before Senate hearings or other groups, one catches glimpses of what is happening in Mexico. For example, Javier Livas, a businessman, stated before a Senate hearing:

Unemployment and underemployment are at record highs, soaring interest rates are hurting individual borrowers, farmers and small businesses and bad loans are piling up at Mexico's increasingly shaky banks. The economic medicine could just end up killing the patient.'[21]

A ten-member delegation of Mexican politicians, business people and academics, meeting US administration officials, said: 'These measures are inspired by the IMF and based on a failed policy . . .'[22] Businessman Ricardo Villa Escalera said: 'Mexico is heading for a major depression.'[23] Gabriel Hinojosa, leader of an independent association of small business, said that the austerity programme is 'designed to destroy the small business sector'.[24]

Mexico's immediate problem is to avoid a crisis of solvency within its financial, industrial and commercial sectors, while at the same time preventing runaway inflation. As a result of these almost unbearable pressures, Mexico faces the risk of serious social disorder.

NAFTA is a typical case of mutual poisoning. Contrary to Lloyd Bentsen's affirmation, the situation is not 'win-win', but 'lose-lose'.

Michel Camdessus, chief executive of the International Monetary Fund, explained that without a bail-out the Mexican crisis would have been 'a world catastrophe'.[25] Financial crises in Latin American countries have been recurring phenomena for many decades. What has suddenly transformed them into potential world catastrophes?

Submarines are built with watertight compartments, so that a leak in one area will not spread and sink the whole vessel. Now that we have globalized the world's economy, the protective compartments no longer exist. Thus, we have globalized problems. A crisis in Mexico has become a 'potential world catastrophe'.

6

The importance of China and India for employment and wages worldwide.

Brian Hindley, 'The Goldsmith Fallacy':

'Chinese GNP is only about 80 per cent of the GNP of Spain ... Relative to the European Union, Japan and the United States, India and China are small economies. Can it really be true that the changes brought about by rapid growth in three or four Spanish-size economies will impoverish and destabilize the industrialized world while at the same time cruelly ravaging the third world (as Sir James predicts on page 15 of *The Trap*)?'

THE RESPONSE

'Chinese GNP is only about 80 per cent of the GNP of Spain.' That is how Hindley reaches the conclusion that the importance of China to the world and its economy is 80 per cent that of Spain.

China is a vast regional superpower with a population of more than 1.2 billion.[1] Its economy is growing extremely fast: its trade surplus with the US alone has risen from about 3 billion dollars in 1986 to nearly 30 billion dollars in 1994.[2] Norman Macrae has pointed out: 'In PPP [purchasing power parity] terms, total GDP of the nearly 1.2 billion mainland Chinese is . . . near 2.9 trillion dollars, making China almost exactly equal with Japan as the world's second biggest economy.'[3] And that was in 1993.

China is determined to recapture its preeminence in Asia and to make itself so strong that it will never again be subjected to perceived slights or indignities from the West. If it keeps itself together, it will become a great world superpower, geopolitically, militarily and economically.

What is more, China's 1.2 billion people (in comparison to Spain's 40 million) represent a huge reservoir of extremely cheap labour. As a result of the continuing exodus from the land into the cities of hundreds of millions of people seeking work, added to the natural growth in population, this reservoir is effectively limitless. The same situation applies in India (population another 919 million people).[4]

THE RESPONSE

Within a system of global free trade which creates a global labour market, the influence of Chinese and Indian labour on earnings and employment worldwide will be overwhelming.

Measuring static situations without understanding either their existing or their future significance is a common disease among conventional economists.

7

The intensive
farming revolution
('the Green Revolution'),
the uprooting of
rural populations and
mass migrations
to urban slums.

The European Commission, document of 19 October 1994:

'The Green Revolution does not create the slums. The migration which swelled urban populations was the result of higher wages in the cities than the countryside. The Green Revolution has, contrary to Sir James's views, helped to reduce these flows by raising rural productivity and, therefore, wages.'

The idea that higher wages in the cities caused the mass migration of farmers away from the land is grotesque. If there were real jobs available in the cities, huge slums consisting of vast quantities of unemployed people would not have grown up all over the world.

NAFTA is an example of the development model which those in the power structures of North America and the European Union seek to impose on societies throughout the world. This model rejects as uneconomic the fact that 26 per cent of the Mexican workforce produces less than 7 per cent of the Gross Domestic Product.[1] The answer, for the supporters of NAFTA and GATT, is surgery – just cut the rural population back to 10 per cent of the workforce. The Mexican Undersecretary of Agriculture has predicted that some 10 million farmers and workers will be chased from the countryside over the next decade.[2]

Where will these people go? The greater Mexico City and Guadalajara areas are already dramatically overpopulated and suffering badly from pollution. How will these NAFTA refugees find employment? Unemployment, which is difficult to measure in Mexico, is already estimated at about 30 per cent. What is more, according to a recent survey conducted in the three largest metropolitan areas, during the first half of 1995 employment fell by 37 per cent in small companies, by 23 per cent in medium-sized companies and by 17 per cent in larger firms.[3] Between 800,000 and one million new people enter the workforce each year.[4] How will they be able to live? There is no money for welfare. Who will supply homes, schools, hospitals, etc.? Contrary to the views of the European Commission, they will, of course, end up in urban slums with all the usual social consequences.

The NAFTA agreement eliminates Mexico's right to national food self-sufficiency and imposes a doctrine according to which Mexico's agricultural system would be complementary to that of the United States. In the process, millions of families will be uprooted and destroyed.

Insofar as 'raising rural productivity and, therefore, wages' is concerned, I have invited Dr José Lutzenberger, former Brazilian Minister of the Environment, and Dr Vandana Shiva, member of the National Environment Council of India and laureate of the Right Livelihood Award (known as the Alternative Nobel Prize), to comment. They are directly in touch on a day-to-day basis with the problems.

Dr Lutzenberger writes:

Modern intensive agriculture, along with the economic policies that reinforce it, are responsible for mass uprooting of small farmers and migrations from the land to the cities.

To suggest that the 'Green Revolution' helped to

reduce these migrations by raising productivity and therefore wages is total nonsense. It fails to take into account that the uprooted peasants were not wage-earners but self-sufficient people.

Let me give you a concrete example. Our foundation has helped peasants move from intensive to organic farming. Today, many of them have incomes, in monetary terms, of less than two hundred dollars a month. In the towns, the man who makes two hundred dollars a month is poor. The farmer who is no longer enslaved to the debts incurred to buy big machines, tractors, combines, chemical fertilizers and pesticides, would not dream of moving to town, even for a higher salary. They pay no rent, no transportation, produce most of their food, have healthy food, don't have to pay for recreation, etc.

The whole economic and technocratic system is geared towards taking away from the farmer all that is really profitable and safe. Instead, the farmer is left with the job of driving tractors, spraying poison, risking his limited capital, facing increased costs for his inputs and falling prices for his products. During the past fifty years, the whole political and economic constellation has been organized to favour the agricultural industrialist at the expense of the farmer. That caused the uprooting. It had the added advantage for industry of supplying cheap labour.

In the Philippines, only the big industrial farms had access to the new methods with their expensive inputs, which in the short term, with the heavy application of chemical fertilizers, produced higher yields. Most small farmers landed in the slums. That is why Manila became the hell it now is.

For the technocrat, a subsistence peasant, even though he might produce enough surplus to feed the cities, is outside the global market economy and therefore does not deserve to survive. The technocrats see those farmers who do manage to survive as being no more than appendages of the large transnational corporations which have become more powerful than governments.[5]

Dr Shiva writes:

The European Commission claim that the Green Revolution raised rural productivity and rural incomes is totally false when the impact of the Green Revolution is viewed from the perspective of the poorer peasants . . .

The Green Revolution did not increase overall biological productivity – it merely increased the yield of globally traded agricultural commodities such as wheat and rice by increasing the dependence of farmers on the application of agricultural chemicals such as pesticides and fertilizers. On the one hand, this has led to a decline in agricultural biodiversity and the availability of diverse crops necessary for the nutrition of farm families, such as pulses, millets and oilseeds. On the other hand, for the poorer families the shift from internal inputs available on the farm (e.g. organic manure) to purchased inputs has led to indebtedness, depeasantization and displacement.

The false productivity of the Green Revolution has been constructed by ignoring the diverse outputs of traditional farming systems and by excluding the economic and ecological costs of the intensive chemicals, intensive irrigation and monocultures associated with the Green Revolution.

When all outputs and all costs of externally purchased inputs are included, the productivity of the Green Revolution is found to be very low. A recent article in *Scientific American*[6] has shown that a traditional Asian polyculture farm uses five units of external inputs to produce 100 units of food output, while a modern Green Revolution farm uses 300 units of purchased inputs to produce 100 units of food output.

Further, when subsidies for chemicals were reduced and higher rates of fertilizers and pesticides had to be applied to maintain yields, there was a falling rate of return even in terms of a market calculus.[7]

THE RESPONSE

Economists count the obvious. They are able to measure that crops can grow faster if certain agro-chemicals are applied. They are also able to calculate that productivity per person employed rises with intensive farming.

But they fail to understand the longer-term, less obvious consequences: the eventual damage to the health and quality of crops; the poisoning of the environment; the diminishing effectiveness of insecticides as insects develop resistance; the cumulative effect on human health of systematically consuming products treated with poisons; the indirect costs to the farmers of buying equipment and chemicals, and so on.

In their calculations economists wholly ignore the effects of chasing people from the land into urban slums. Of course, the social cost of uprooting and destroying tens of millions of families does not lend itself to economic measurement. The suffering, of individuals and of society, is too deep and too extensive.

8

All economic activity
is not productive.

The European Commission, document of 19 October 1994:

'All economic activity, by definition, is productive.'

THE RESPONSE

This belief that all economic activity is productive is at the heart of the problems that society faces.

Economic activity is measured officially by the index of Gross National Product. Let me quote from the opening chapter of my book, *The Trap:*

But GNP measures only activity. It measures neither prosperity nor well-being. For example, if a calamity occurs, such as a hurricane or an earthquake, the immediate consequence is a growth in GNP because activity is increased so as to repair the damage. If a great epidemic hits a community, GNP grows as the result of the construction of new hospitals and the employment of public health workers. If the crime rate increases, GNP grows as more police join the force and new prisons are built. We can take this even further. The cost of cancer in America is estimated at 110 billion dollars per annum,[1] equal to 1.7 per cent of GNP; the cost of drug abuse is 200 billion dollars,[2] or 3.1 per cent of GNP; the cost of crime is 163 billion dollars,[3] or 2.6 per cent of GNP. These three areas alone contribute 473 billion dollars, 7.4 per cent, to the nation's GNP and they are all growing.

The politicians and technocrats who govern us are unable to understand why the enormous growth in economic activity during the past decades has led to rising unemployment, increasing poverty and spreading urban slums. They cannot accept that the growth that they are promoting is tumescent and malignant. They believe that the sicknesses which afflict our society – growth in crime, drug abuse, alcoholism, family breakdown, civil disorder, environmental degradation – are no more than the normal phenomena which inevitably accompany economic development and progress. So they concentrate their political, economic and social programmes on initiatives whose principal purpose is to make GNP grow quantitatively, without regard to its impact on society. They find it difficult to distinguish between a nation and a commercial enterprise. Often, they describe their own country as though it were a company, for example, UK plc.

David de Pury, Switzerland's former chief negotiator in the Uruguay Round of GATT, and now chairman of the transnational company Asea Brown Boveri, even suggests that transnational companies should have 'direct access' to the workings of the World Trade Organization, the body set up following the recent Uruguay Round to regulate world trade. 'Would it make sense,' de Pury asks, 'to start thinking of a system more adapted to the fact that multinational companies have become the main constituency of the trading system?'[4]

De Pury's use of the words 'main constituency' takes for granted the preeminence of the interests of multinational companies rather than those of society as a whole, in a free world economy. This accurately reflects the belief of our power elites. The world economy is to be run for the benefit of footloose corporations, not to serve the fundamental requirements of communities throughout the world.

We know that there are now two different and conflicting economies, the corporate economy and the national economy. Is society going to continue to accept that its true needs are subservient to the interests of the corporate economy? Or will we bring harmony to the two, so that they both prosper within a home economy respectful of free enterprise?

9

The illustrated story of global free trade.

CHART 1

Over 4 billion people in
low-wage countries enter
the free world's economy.

WORLD POPULATION FORECASTS 1990-2020
(in millions)

	1990	2000	2010	2020
World	5284	6158	7032	7888
Developed	1143	1186	1213	1232
Less developed	4141	4972	5819	6656
Africa	633	832	1069	1348
Asia	3186	3736	4264	4744
Western Europe	403	415	417	414
Eastern Europe	170	169	169	169
Latin America[1]	440	524	604	676
North America	278	306	332	358
Oceania	26	31	35	39
Former USSR	148	146	143	140

[1]The figure for Latin America includes Mexico.

Source: United Nations.

CHART 2

Their salaries are very, very low.
For example, 47 workers in
the Philippines or in Vietnam can
be employed for the cost of a
single worker in France.

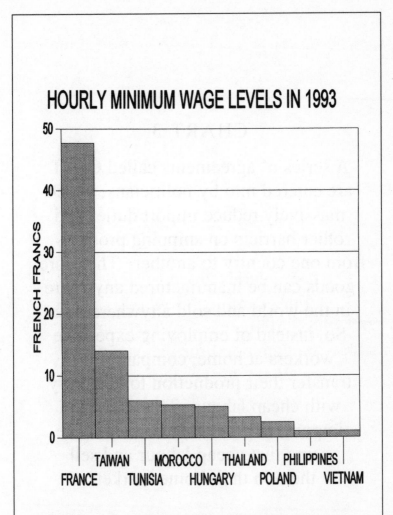

HOURLY MINIMUM WAGE LEVELS IN 1993

FRENCH FRANCS

50
40
30
20
10
0

FRANCE
TAIWAN
TUNISIA
MOROCCO
HUNGARY
THAILAND
POLAND
PHILIPPINES
VIETNAM

Source: *French Senate Finance Committee and Direction des Relations Economiques Extérieures.*

CHART 3

A series of agreements called GATT
are entered into by politicians, which
massively reduce import duties and
other barriers on shipping products
from one country to another. Therefore,
goods can be manufactured anywhere
in the world and sold anywhere else.
So, instead of employing expensive
workers at home, companies can
transfer their production to a country
with cheap labour. Then they will
import the products that they make
using that cheap labour and sell
them in their home markets.

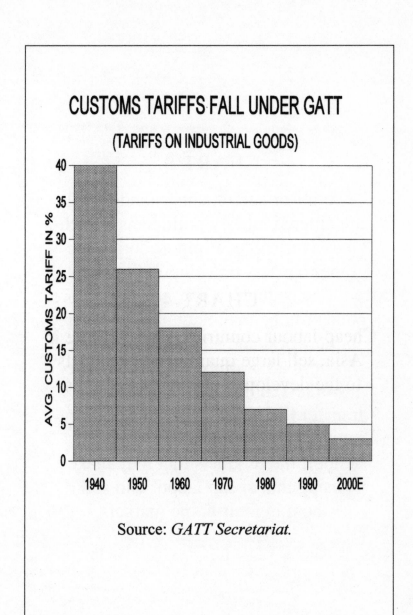

CUSTOMS TARIFFS FALL UNDER GATT

(TARIFFS ON INDUSTRIAL GOODS)

Source: *GATT Secretariat.*

CHART 4

Cheap-labour countries, such as those in Asia, sell large quantities of products to the developed countries, i.e. to us.

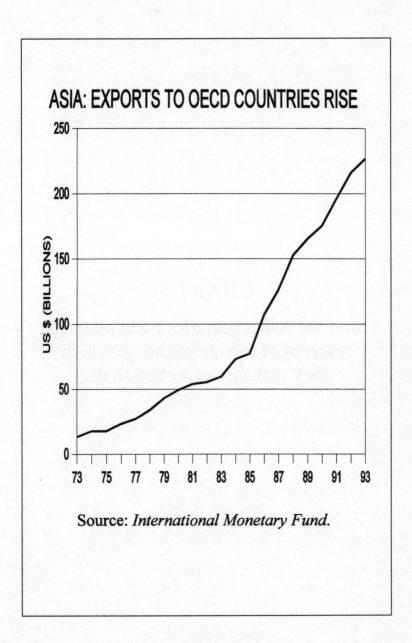

ASIA: EXPORTS TO OECD COUNTRIES RISE

Source: *International Monetary Fund.*

CHART 5

And the Asian countries build up huge reserves of foreign exchange which they make by exporting to us.

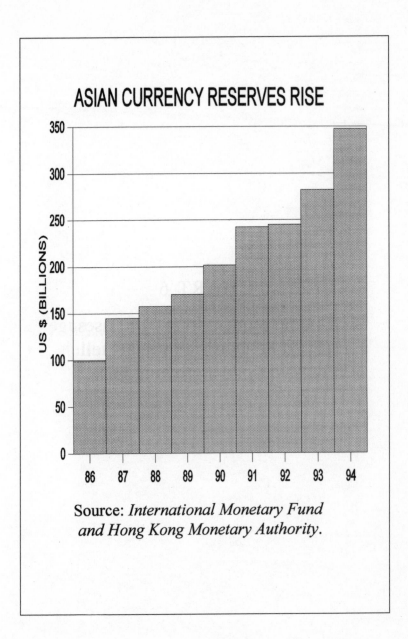

ASIAN CURRENCY RESERVES RISE

Source: *International Monetary Fund
and Hong Kong Monetary Authority.*

CHART 6

Unemployment in the UK rises
(by more than the officials tell
us) – despite a growing GDP.

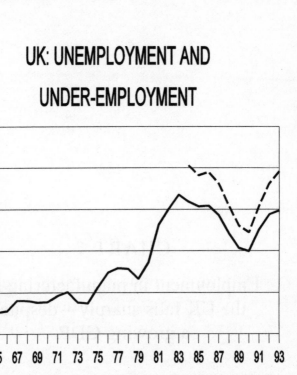

UK: UNEMPLOYMENT AND UNDER-EMPLOYMENT

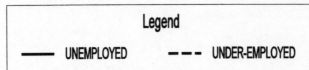

Source: *Organization for Economic
Cooperation and Development.*

CHART 7

Employment in manufacturing in
the UK falls sharply – despite
a growing GDP.

UK: EMPLOYMENT IN MANUFACTURING
FALLS AS GDP RISES

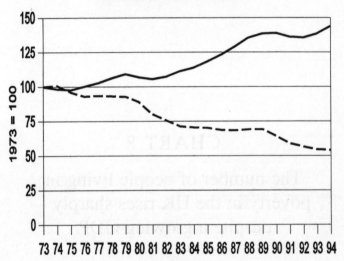

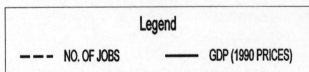

Source: *UK Department of Education and Employment, and the International Monetary Fund.*

CHART 8

The number of people living in poverty in the UK rises sharply – despite a growing GDP.

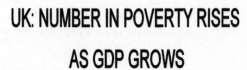

UK: NUMBER IN POVERTY RISES
AS GDP GROWS

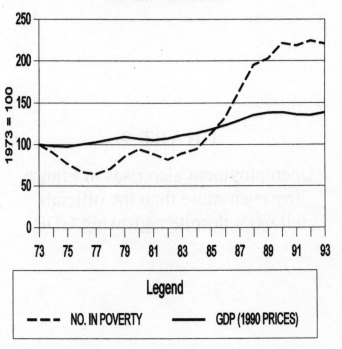

Source: *UK Department of Social Security,
and the International Monetary Fund.*

CHART 9

Unemployment also rises in France
(by even more than the officials
tell us) – despite a growing GDP.

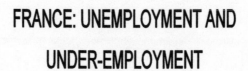

FRANCE: UNEMPLOYMENT AND UNDER-EMPLOYMENT

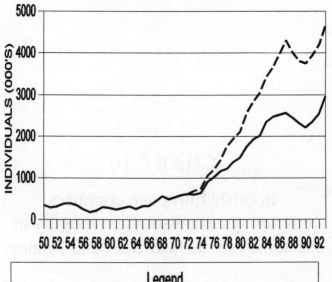

Source: *Allais, M.,* Combats pour L'Europe:1992-94.

CHART 10

In other European countries
unemployment also rises, roughly at
the same rate as in Britain and France.

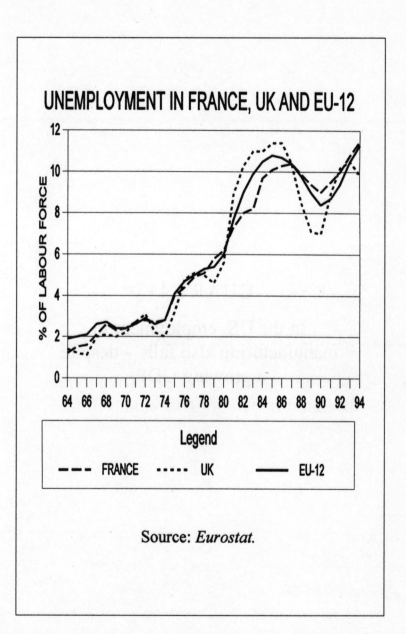

UNEMPLOYMENT IN FRANCE, UK AND EU-12

Legend

--- FRANCE ····· UK ——— EU-12

Source: *Eurostat.*

CHART 11

In the US, employment in manufacturing also falls – despite a growing GDP.

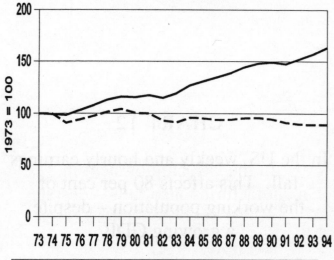

US: EMPLOYMENT IN MANUFACTURING
FALLS AS GDP RISES

$1973 = 100$

73 74 75 76 77 78 79 80 81 82 83 84 85 86 87 88 89 90 91 92 93 94

Legend

– – – NO. OF JOBS ——— GDP (1990 PRICES)

Source: *US Bureau of Labor Statistics,
and the International Monetary Fund.*

CHART 12

In the US, weekly and hourly earnings
fall. This affects 80 per cent of
the working population – despite
a growing GDP.

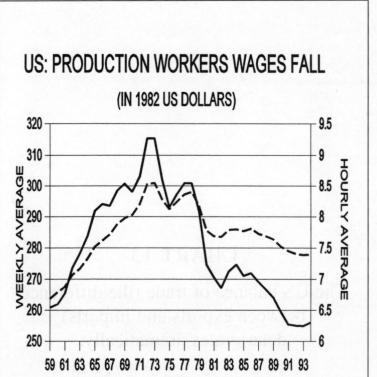

US: PRODUCTION WORKERS WAGES FALL

(IN 1982 US DOLLARS)

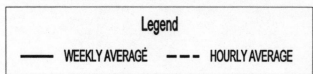

Source: *US Department of Labor,*
Bureau of Labor Statistics.

CHART 13

The US balance of trade (the difference between exports and imports) deteriorates dramatically.

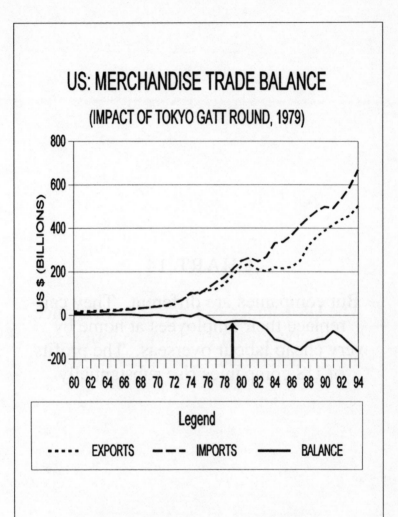

US: MERCHANDISE TRADE BALANCE

(IMPACT OF TOKYO GATT ROUND, 1979)

US $ (BILLIONS)

800

600

400

200

0

-200

60 62 64 66 68 70 72 74 76 78 80 82 84 86 88 90 92 94

Legend

····· EXPORTS   ─ ─ ─ IMPORTS   ──── BALANCE

Source: *US Department of Commerce*.

CHART 14

But companies are different. They can replace their employees at home by very cheap labour overseas. The profits of US companies rise substantially.

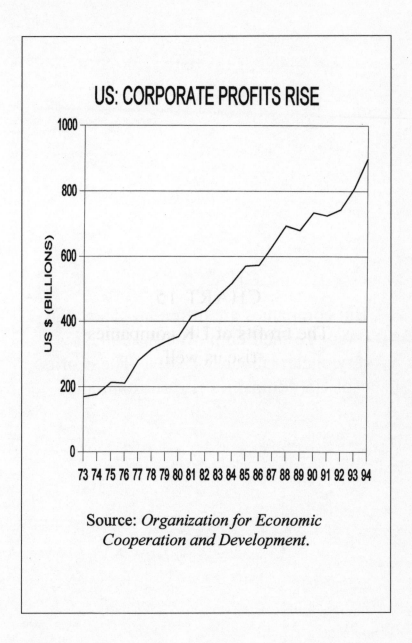

US: CORPORATE PROFITS RISE

Source: *Organization for Economic Cooperation and Development*.

CHART 15

The profits of UK companies
rise as well.

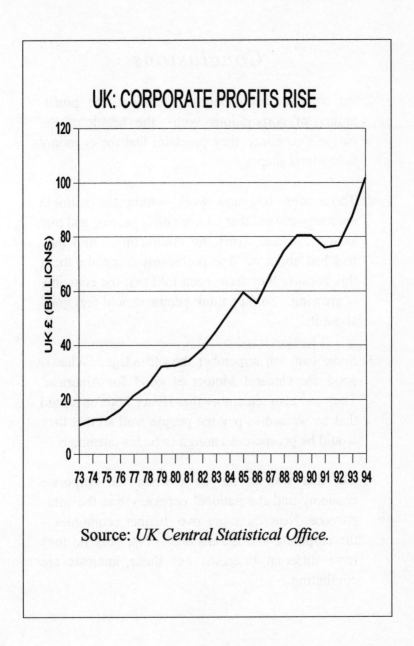

UK: CORPORATE PROFITS RISE

Source: *UK Central Statistical Office.*

Conclusions

1. As conventional economists confuse the profitability of corporations with the health of the nation's economy, they proclaim that the economy is in sound shape.

2. Those who live and work within the national economy can see that jobs are disappearing and that salaries, in real terms, are contracting. And they feel bad about it. The politicians complain about this because they have been told that the economy is growing. So they think people should feel good about it.

3. Some can still remember the old adage: 'What is good for General Motors is good for America.' They can also remember that Henry Ford once said that he wanted to pay his people well so that they would be prosperous enough to be his customers.

4. But that was in the days when the corporate economy and the national economy had the same purpose. Now there are two distinct economies – the corporate and the national. Not only do they have different interests, but those interests are conflicting.

5. As corporations switch production to the areas with the cheapest labour and then import the products made abroad, they destroy jobs at home and increase the nation's trade deficit.

6. Conventional economists try to soothe us by saying things like: 'Nor does a glance at the statistics of trade suggest that trade with the developing countries has caused, or could have caused, significant unemployment in the European Union' (Brian Hindley). Or they say, 'To summarize, trade with low-wage ecomomies does not cause major reductions in total employment or real earnings' (the European Commission).

7. They even say that it does not matter if our trade deficits bankrupts us as we will borrow the money to pay (the European Commission, et al).

   That is the way to national suicide – unless the resulting social disorder forces change onto those who would impose on society their conventional wisdom.

Notes

NOTES

CHAPTER ONE

1. *World Population Prospects: The 1994 Revision,* New York: United Nations, 1994.
2. Ricardo, D., *On the Principles of Political Economy and Taxation,* Harmondsworth: Penguin, 1971 (first published 1817), p. 155.
3. *World Debt Tables: 1994-95,* Washington: World Bank, 1995. The figures are for net resource flows (long-term) which are the sum of net resource flows on long-term-debt (excluding the IMF) plus non-debt-creating flows. These latter flows include foreign direct investment, portfolio investment, and official grants. Long-term loans are expressed net of repayments.
4. Figures produced by the Asia-Pacific Economics Group at the Australian National University and due to be published in Rohwer, J., *Asia Rising,* New York: Simon and Schuster, 1995. East Asian countries referred to in the chart are China, Hong Kong, Indonesia, Japan, Korea, Malaysia, Philippines, Singapore, Thailand, Taiwan and Vietnam.
5. Hindley in The 'Goldsmith Fallacy' states that I have 'been misled'. Hindley asserts that: 'When Ricardo discusses comparative advantage as such, he never uses monetary terms.' I refer Hindley to Ricardo's chapter on foreign trade in which he writes: 'If by the purchase of English goods to the amount of £1,000, a merchant can obtain a quantity of foreign goods, which he can sell in the English market for £1,200, he will obtain 20 per cent profit by such an employment of his capital' (Ricardo, 1971:147). I would further refer Hindley to pages 149-150; 156-158,

NOTES

and 165-167 of the same chapter. The value of a comparative advantage in an international trading system must inevitably be valued in money terms.

6. Keynes, J.M., 'National Self-Sufficiency', in *The Collected Writings of John Maynard Keynes, Vol. 21*, D. Moggeridge (ed.), London: Macmillan and Cambridge University Press, 1982.

CHAPTER TWO

1. 'Cost of protection: Trade barriers spawn more trade barriers', *San Diego Union*, 30 April 1985.

2. *World Population Prospects: The 1994 Revision*, New York: United Nations, 1994.

3. *Republic of China Yearbook 1995*, Taiwan: Government Information Office, 1995.

4. *International Financial Statistics*, Washington: International Monetary Fund, July 1995.

5. Payer, C., *Lent and Lost, Foreign Credit and Third World Development*, London and New Jersey: Zed Books Ltd., 1991.

6. Hobsbawm, E., *Industry and Empire*, Harmondsworth: Penguin, 1969, p. 140. 'The USA was the only major economic power which remained systematically protectionist' during the nineteenth century.

7. Bairoch, P., *Economics and World History: Myths and Paradoxes,* London: Harvester Wheatsheaf, 1993, p. 40. The average tariff rates on manufactured products (weighted average, in percentage of value), applied by the

NOTES

US in 1820, 1875 and 1913 are estimated at: 35-45 per cent; 40-50 per cent; and 44 per cent.

8. Bairoch, P., *Mythes et paradoxes de l'histoire economique*, Paris: Editions de la Découverte, 1995.

9. *Ibid.*

10. Parker, W., *Europe, America and the Wider World, Essays on the Economic History of Western Capitalism, Vol. 2: America and the Wider World*, Cambridge: Cambridge University Press, 1991, p. 11. 'As America's own manufacturers, protected by the Republican tariffs, replaced European manufacturers, the mix of imports shifted toward truly luxurious consumer goods and producer goods embodying high technology.'

11. Press conference on Europe by General de Gaulle, held at the Elysée Palace, 14 January 1963.

12. The Smoot–Hawley Tariff Act was sponsored by Senator Reed Smoot (R–Utah) and Congressman Willis C. Hawley (R–Oregon).

13. Vice-President Al Gore, debating NAFTA with Ross Perot on *Larry King Live,* CNN, 9 November 1993.

14. US Department of Labor, Bureau of Labor Statistics, *Employment and Earnings*, Washington: Government Printing Office, January 1987.

15. Lloyd, L., *Tariffs: The Case for Protection*, New York: Devin Adair, 1955, p. 181.

16. Bedell Associates: *Smoot–Hawley, Depression and World Revolution*, Palm Desert, California: Bedell Associates, April 1983. Reproduced in the *Congressional Record*, 9 May 1983, p. 11539.

NOTES

17. *Ibid.*
18. *Ibid.*
19. *Ibid.*
20. Bairoch, P., *Mythes et paradoxes de l'histoire economique*, Paris: Editions de la Découverte, 1995.
21. Senator Heinz's speech can be found in the *Congressional Record*, 9 May 1983, p. 11538.
22. Bedell Associates, *op. cit.*
23. Bairoch, P., *Mythes et paradoxes de l'histoire economique*, Paris: Editions de la Découverte, 1995.
24. *Main Economic Indicators*, Paris: Organization for Economic Cooperation and Development, August 1995.
25. Tonelson, A., 'Beating Back Predatory Trade', *Foreign Affairs*, Vol. 73, No. 4, July 1994.

CHAPTER TWO, APPENDIX A

1. 'Awash in a sea of money', *Far Eastern Economic Review*, Hong Kong, 15 September 1988, p. 49-70.
2. *Economic News*, Taiwan, 4-10 July 1983.
3. Tsiang, S., and Chen, W., 'Developments towards trade liberalization in Taiwan', paper presented at the joint conference on the industrial policies of the ROC and ROK, Chung-Hua Institution for Economic Research, Taipei, 28 December 1984.
4. Wade, R., *Governing the Market: Economic Theory and the Role of Government in East Asian Industrialization*, Princeton: Princeton University Press, 1990, p.131.

NOTES

5. Tu, C., and Wang, W., 'Trade liberalization in the Republic of China on Taiwan, and the economic effects of tariff reductions', paper presented at the joint conference on the industrial policies of the ROC and the ROK, Korea Development Institute, January 1988.

6. Cited in Scott, M., 'Foreign Trade', in W. Galenson (ed.), *Economic Growth and Structural Change in Taiwan: The Postwar Experience of the Republic of China*, Ithaca: Cornell University Press, 1979.

7. Lin, C., *Industrialization in Taiwan, 1946-72: Trade and Import-Substitution Policies for Developing Countries*, New York: Praeger, 1973.

8. Wade, R., *op. cit.*

9. Lee, C., *The Economic Transformation of South Korea – Lessons for Economies in the Process of Change*, Paris: Organization for Economic Cooperation and Development, 1995.

10. *Korea: Managing the Industrial Transition*, Washington: World Bank, Vols. 1 and 2, 1987.

11. Wade, R., *op. cit.*

12. Westphal, L., and Kim, K., 'Korea', in B. Balassa, et al. (eds.), *Development Strategies in Semi-Industrial Economies*, Baltimore: Johns Hopkins University Press for the World Bank, 1982.

13. Young, S., 'Trade policy reform in Korea: background and prospect', paper presented at the joint conference on industrial policies of ROC and ROK, Korea Development Institute, 1984.

14. Wade, R., *op. cit.*

NOTES

CHAPTER TWO, APPENDIX B

1. Figures are taken from Tonelson. A., 'Beating Back Predatory Trade', in *Foreign Affairs,* Vol. 73, No. 4, July 1994.

CHAPTER THREE

1. Allais, M., *Combats pour l'Europe, 1992-94*, Paris: Clement Juglar, 1995.
2. *Ibid.*
3. 'Recent labour market developments and prospects' and 'Supplementary measures of labour market slack', in *Employment Outlook*, Paris: Organization for Economic Cooperation and Development, July 1995.
4. *Report of the Working Party on the Measurement of Unemployment in the UK*, London: Royal Statistical Society, April 1995.
5. Sorrentino, C., 'International comparisons of unemployment indicators', *Monthly Labor Review*, Washington: US Department of Labor, March 1993.
6. Allais, M., *op. cit.*
7. *Ibid.*
8. Council of Economic Advisors, *Economic Report of the President 1995*, Washington: Government Printing Office, February 1995, Table B-45. (Data from Bureau of Labor Statistics.)
9. Mishel, L., and Bernstein, J., *The State of Working America: 1994-1995*, Armonk: M.E. Sharpe for the Economic Policy Institute, 1994. The same analysis of American underemployment was made by Dr Herman

NOTES

Starobin of the International Ladies Garment Workers Union, in his evidence on the impact of GATT, presented to the US Senate Committee on Labor and Human Resources, 23 November 1994.

10. Council of Economic Advisors, *op. cit.*, Table B-47.
11. *Ibid.*, Table B-45.
12. *World Tables 1994*, Baltimore: Johns Hopkins University Press for the World Bank, 1994. Plus update diskettes.
13. *World Employment 1995,* Geneva: International Labour Organization, 1995.
14. *World Labour Report*, Geneva: International Labour Organization, 1992.
15. 'Who's in Charge Here', *Newsweek*, 26 June 1995.

CHAPTER THREE, APPENDIX

1. 'Skilled workers watch their jobs migrate overseas', *New York Times*, 28 August 1995.
2. *Multinational Corporations: Expanding Influence in the 1990s*, Washington: AFL – CIO Economic Research Department, February 1995.
3. The BEM's are Argentina, Brazil, China, Hong Kong, India, Indonesia, South Korea, Mexico, Poland, South Africa, Taiwan and Turkey.
4. 'US trade losses with "Big Emerging Markets" surge toward new record in 1995', news release from MBG Information Services, Washington, 21 July 1995.
5. 'Germany's economy is a "Wund" for the wrong reasons', *Wall Street Journal Europe*, Brussels, 25 July 1995.

6. 'Job competition and pressure on wages begin to reach America's labor elite', *Wall Street Journal Europe*, Brussels, 30 September 1994.
7. *Ibid.*
8. 'S. Korea discovers joys of investing in China', *Financial Times*, London, 23 August 1995.
9. 'Europe's Labors: Integrating the East, Reinventing the West are one and the same', *Wall Street Journal Europe*, Brussels, 30 June 1995.
10. French Senate Finance Commission, *Rapport d'information du Sénat sur les délocalisations hors du territoire national des activités industrielles et de service'*, 4 June 1993.
11. Figures for 1994 from Union Française des Industries de l'Habillement et Union des Industries Textiles.
12. Figures for 1994 from Fédération Française de l'Industrie de la Chaussure de France.
13. Figures for 1994 from Chambre Française de l'Horlogerie et des Microtechniques.
14. Figures for 1994 from Syndicat des Industries de Matériels Audiovisuels Electroniques.

CHAPTER FOUR

1. 'Financial Indicators', *Economist,* London, 5 November 1994.
2. 'Paying for the Foreign Debts', *Washington Post*, final edition, 3 November 1994.
3. The figures for general government gross financial liabilities can be found in *OECD Economic Outlook*, Paris: Organization for Economic Cooperation and Development,

December 1994. The figures on net pension liabilities are taken from *OECD Economic Surveys – Japan*, Paris: Organization for Economic Cooperation and Development, 1994, *OECD Economic Surveys – Belgium/Luxembourg*, Paris: Organization for Economic Cooperation and Development, 1994.

4.   The G7 nations are Canada, France, Germany, Italy, Japan, the United Kingdom and the United States.

5.   'Belgium's Debt Crisis is Europe's Too', *Wall Street Journal Europe*, Brussels, 22 May 1995.

6.   *Ibid.*

7.   *Wall Street Journal Europe, op. cit.*

8.   'The Coming Chinese Money Mountain', *Asia Inc.*, Hong Kong, September 1993.

CHAPTER FIVE

1.   *World Population Prospects: The 1994 Revision*, New York: United Nations, 1994.

2.   *Main Economic Indicators*, Paris: Organization for Economic Cooperation and Development, August 1995.

3.   'Portugal Seeks Place In Another New World: The Global Economy', *Wall Street Journal Europe,* Brussels, 28 June 1995.

4.   *Ibid.*

5.   United Nations, *op. cit.*

6.   'Happy Ever NAFTA?', *Economist,* London, 10 December 1994.

7.   *International Financial Statistics,* Washington: International Monetary Fund, various editions.

NOTES

8. Senator Dorgan's speech appears in the *Congressional Record,* 12 June 1995.

9. Scott, R., *1994 and 1995, US–Mexico Trade Data: NAFTA Impact,* Occasional Paper No. 56, Business Center for International Education and Research, University of Maryland, May 1995.

10. MBG Information Services, Washington, using FT900 Series from US Bureau of Census..

11. Senator Dorgan, *op. cit.*

12. Scott, R., *op. cit.*

13. MBG Information Services, *op. cit.*

14. 'US Pitches Unilateral Aid for Mexico But Lawmakers Foresee a Hard Sell', *Washington Post,* 26 January 1995.

15. Chemical Bank Emerging Markets Research, *Latin American Economic Outlook,* New York, May 1995.

16. 'Mexico's Depression Deepening', news release from MBG Information Services, Washington, 22 August 1995.

17. Mexico's National Development Bank (NAFIN), *The Stock Market,* Mexico City, English edition, July/August 1995.

18. 'Mexico's Depression Deepening', news release from MBG Information Services, Washington, 22 August 1995.

19. Mexican Treasury, *Report on the Status of the Economy, Public Finances, and Public Debt,* Mexico City, August 1995.

20. 'Mexico's Depression Deepening', news release from MBG Information Services, Washington, 22 August 1995.

21. 'Mexicans, Americans call rescue a disaster', *Washington Times,* 25 May 1995.

NOTES

22. 'Mexican delegation, decrying economic remedy as "Worse than the sickness," meets with Washington policymakers', press release from The Development Gap, Washington, 19 April 1995.
23. 'Mexico Economy Worsening, Group Says', news release from United Press International, Washington, 21 April 1995.
24. *Ibid*.
25. 'Camdessus: crise Méxique aurait été «une catastrophe mondiale» sans aide', dispatch number 192/193 from Agence France Presse, 2 February 1995.

CHAPTER SIX

1. *World Population Prospects: The 1994 Revision*, New York: United Nations, 1994.
2. 'US trade losses to China exceed 100 billion dollars since democratic crackdown', news release from MBG Information Services, Washington, based on data from US Department of Commerce and the Bureau of Census, 31 May 1995.
3. 'The Coming Chinese Money Mountain', *Asia Inc.*, Hong Kong, September 1993.
4. United Nations, *op. cit*.

CHAPTER SEVEN

1. Navarro, L.H., 'The GATT Agreement and Agriculture: Will it help Developing Countries?', paper presented at a

167

seminar organized by the Catholic Institute for International Relations, London, 12 April 1994.

2. Alliance for Responsible Trade, *NAFTA's First Year: Lessons for the Hemisphere,* Washington, December 1994.

3. 'Mexico's Depression Deepening', news release from MBG Information Services, Washington, 22 August 1995.

4. INEGI, *Advanced Report on the Economy*, Mexico City, June 1995.

5. Personal communication to the author, 16 August 1995.

6. Bray, F., 'Agriculture for Developing Nations', *Scientific American*, New York, July 1994.

7. Personal communication to the author, 11 August 1995.

CHAPTER EIGHT

1. 'What About "Putting People First"?', *Los Angeles Times,* 8 September 1993.

2. Godson, R., and Olson, W., *International Organized Crime: Emerging Threat to US Security,* Washington: National Strategy Information Center, August 1993.

3. 'A Murder Shows the Crushing Cost of US Crime', *Washington Post,* 6 July 1994.

4. 'The New Multilateral Trading System Needs Urgent Attention', *International Herald Tribune,* Paris, 23 August 1995.

CHAPTER NINE

1. *World Population Prospects: The 1994 Revision,* New York: United Nations, 1994.

NOTES

2. French Senate Finance Commission, *Rapport d'information du Sénat sur les délocalisations hors du territoire national des activités industrielles et de service'*, 4 June 1993. The figures appear on page 23 of the report and were produced by the Postes d'Expansion Economique, the Direction des Relations Economiques Extérieures, and the Senate Finance Commission.

3. Figures provided by the GATT Secretariat in Geneva.

4. *Direction of Trade Statistics,* Washington: International Monetary Fund, various editions. In the graph the OECD countries shown do not include Turkey or Mexico. The Asian countries are China, India, Korea, Philippines, Taiwan, Thailand and Vietnam.

5. *International Financial Statistics,* Washington: International Monetary Fund, various editions. Hong Kong Monetary Authority, *Monthly Statistical Bulletin,* Hong Kong, July 1995. The Asian countries represented in the graph are China, Hong Kong, Indonesia, Korea, Malaysia, Singapore, Taiwan, Thailand. The figures include reserves of gold and Special Drawing Rights, except for Hong Kong, where only foreign exchange reserves are included.

6. The figures for UK unemployment come from the Statistics Division of the Organization for Economic Cooperation and Development, and are derived from the harmonized unemployment rate data published in various editions of *Labour Force Statistics*. The underemployment figure is calculated by adding the total number of 'discouraged workers' and 'involuntary part-time workers' to the official ILO unemployment figures. The data on discouraged and involuntary part-time workers can be found in

NOTES

'Supplementary measures of labour market slack', in *Employment Outlook,* Paris: Organization for Economic Cooperation and Development, July 1995.

7. The data on the number of employees in manufacturing comes from Division SSD D2 of the UK Department of Education and Employment, and relates to 'manufacturing employees as a percentage of the total workforce in employment.' The United Kingdom's GDP at 1990 prices is taken from *International Financial Statistics,* Washington: International Monetary Fund, various editions.

8. The number of individuals living on less than 50% of average income can be found in *Households Below Average Income,* published by Her Majesty's Stationery Office for the Department of Social Security in London. Figures through to 1991 are presented in Goodman, A., and Webb, S., *For Richer, For Poorer,* London: Institute for Fiscal Studies, Commentary No. 42, 1994. GDP figures from IMF as in note 7 above.

9. Allais, M., *Combats pour l'Europe, 1992-94,* Paris: Clement Juglar, 1995, p. 494.

10. Commission of the European Communities, *European Economy,* Brussels: Directorate General for Economic and Financial Affairs, No. 58, 1994.

11. The employment figures relate to employees on non-agricultural payrolls in manufacturing industries, and can be found in Council of Economic Advisors, *Economic Report of the President,* Washington: Government Printing Office, February 1995, Table

170

NOTES

B-47. The number of employees in manufacturing has declined gradually since 1973, but during this period the size of the American workforce has increased substantially. If the graph showed manufacturing employees as a percentage of the workforce, then the downward trend would be much more marked. GDP figures for the United States at 1990 prices come from the IMF (as in note 7 above).

12. Data on the hourly and weekly wages of production and non-supervisory workers (in 1982 dollars) can be found in Council of Economic Advisors, *op. cit.*, Table B-45. (Data from Bureau of Labor Statistics.)

13. *Survey of Current Business*, Washington: Bureau of Economic Analysis, Department of Commerce, various editions.

14. The figures are for the gross trading profits of non-financial enterprises and can be found in *Non-Financial Enterprises, Financial Statements*, Paris: Organization for Economic Cooperation and Development, various editions.

15. Data are supplied by the UK Central Statistical Office, and relate to non-financial corporations in the private sector, showing gross trading profits including stock appreciation.

Appendix

The New Utopia: GATT and global free trade

reproduced from

The Trap

published November 1994

THE NEW UTOPIA:

The Trap was first published as *Le Piège* in France in 1993 and was based on conversations with Yves Messarovitch, editor of the Economics section of *Le Figaro*.

GATT AND GLOBAL FREE TRADE

You are opposed to global free trade and therefore to GATT. Why?

Global free trade has become a sacred principle of modern economic theory, a sort of generally accepted moral dogma. That is why it is so difficult to persuade politicians and economists to reassess its effects on a world economy which is changing radically.

The ultimate objective of global free trade is to create a worldwide market in products, services, capital and labour. Its instrument to achieve this is GATT, the General Agreement on Tariffs and Trade.

I believe that GATT and the theories on which it is based are flawed. If it is implemented, it will impoverish and destabilize the industrialized world while at the same time cruelly ravaging the third world.

Remind us of the economic theory on which GATT is based.

The principal theoretician of free trade was David Ricardo, a British economist of the early nineteenth century.[1] He believed in two interrelated concepts: specialization and comparative advantage. According to Ricardo, each nation should specialize in those activities in which it excels, so that it can have the greatest advantage relative to other countries. Thus, a nation should narrow its focus of activity, abandoning certain industries and developing those in which it has the largest

175

comparative advantage. As a result, international trade would grow as nations export their surpluses and import the products that they no longer manufacture, efficiency and productivity would increase in line with economies of scale and prosperity would be enhanced. But these ideas are not valid in today's world.

Why?

During the past few years, 4 billion people have suddenly entered the world economy. They include the populations of China, India, Vietnam, Bangladesh, and the countries that were part of the Soviet empire, among others. These populations are growing fast; in thirty-five years, that 4 billion is forecast to expand to over 6.5 billion.[2] These nations have very high levels of unemployment and those people who do find jobs offer their labour for a tiny fraction of the pay earned by workers in the developed world. For example, forty-seven Vietnamese or forty-seven Filipinos can be employed for the cost of one person in the developed world, such as France.[3]

Until recently, these 4 billion people were separated from our economy by their political systems, primarily communist or socialist, and because of a lack of technology and of capital. Today all that has changed. Their political systems have been transformed, technology can be transferred instantaneously anywhere in the world on a microchip, and capital is free to be invested wherever the anticipated yields are highest.

GATT AND GLOBAL FREE TRADE

The principle of global free trade is that anything can be manufactured anywhere in the world to be sold anywhere else. That means that these new entrants into the world economy are in direct competition with the workforces of developed countries. They have become part of the same global labour market. Our economies, therefore, will be subjected to a completely new type of competition. For example, take two enterprises, one in the developed world and one in Vietnam. Both make an identical product destined to be sold in the same market, say the USA, Great Britain or France; both can use identical technology; both have access to the same pool of international capital. The only difference is that the Vietnamese enterprise can employ forty-seven people where the French enterprise can employ only one. You don't have to be a genius to understand who will be the winner in such a contest.

In most developed nations, the cost to an average manufacturing company of paying its workforce is an amount equal to between 25 per cent and 30 per cent of sales. If such a company decides to maintain in its home country only its head office and sales force, while transferring its production to a low-cost area, it will save about 20 per cent of sales volume. Thus, a company with sales of 500 million dollars will increase its pre-tax profits by up to 100 million dollars every year. If, on the other hand, it decides to maintain its production at home, the enterprise will be unable to compete with low-cost imports and will perish.

THE NEW UTOPIA:

It must surely be a mistake to adopt an economic policy which makes you rich if you eliminate your national workforce and transfer production abroad, and which bankrupts you if you continue to employ your own people.

But the companies that move offshore are those which employ large labour forces. Surely the new jobs that will be created by the high-tech industries of the future will compensate.

High-tech industries can, indeed, survive and prosper under these circumstances, for the very reason that they are highly automated and therefore employ few people. Labour is no more than a minor item in the overall cost of the products they make. But obviously they cannot compensate for the lost manufacturing jobs: the fact that they employ few people means that they are incapable of employing very many. As soon as they need to employ a reasonable number, they will be forced to move offshore. For example, IBM is moving its disk-drive business from America and Western Europe to low-labour-cost countries. According to the *Wall Street Journal*: 'IBM plans to establish this new site as a joint venture with an undetermined Asian partner and use non-IBM employees so that it will be easier . . . to move to an even lower-cost region when warranted . . . Moving from higher-cost regions to Asia cuts in half the cost of assembling a disk drive.' Mr Zschau of IBM 'admitted that the moves will put IBM on only even footing with its competitors'.[4] The aircraft manufacturer Boeing has announced that it will transfer some of its production to China.[5] The sort of companies that created Silicon Valley, like Hewlett-Packard and Advanced Micro Devices, are also shifting employment to low-wage countries.[6]

Proponents of global free trade constantly say that exporting such high-tech products as very fast trains, airplanes and satellites will create jobs on a large scale. Alas, this is not true. The recent 2.1 billion dollar contract selling very fast French trains to South Korea has resulted in the maintenance, for four years, of only 800 jobs in France: 525 for the main supplier and 275 for the subcontractors.[7] Much of the work is carried out in Korea by Asian companies using Asian labour. What is more, following the transfer of technology to South Korea, in a few years' time Asia will be able to buy very fast trains directly from South Korea and bypass France. As for planes and satellites, the numbers employed in this industry in France have fallen steadily. Over the five years from 1987 to 1992, they have declined from 123,000 to 111,000 and are forecast to fall to 102,000 in the short term.[8]

One of the big mistakes that we make is that when we talk about balancing trade we think exclusively in monetary terms. If we export one billion dollars' worth of goods and import products of the same value, we conclude that our overseas trade is in balance. The value of our exports is equal to that of our imports. But this is a superficial analysis and leads to wrong conclusions. The products that we export must necessarily be those which use only a small amount of labour. If not, they would be unable to compete with products manufactured in low-labour-cost countries and so would be unexportable. The number of people employed annually to produce one billion dollars' worth of high-tech products in the developed nations could be under a thousand. But the number of people employed in the low-cost areas to manufacture the goods that we import would be in the tens of thousands, because these are not high-tech products but ones produced with traditional levels of employment. So, our trade might be in balance in monetary terms, but if we look beyond the monetary figures we find that there is a terrible imbalance in terms of employment. That is how we export jobs and import unemployment.

But many economists believe that the growth in service industries will compensate for lost jobs in manufacturing.

Even service industries will be subjected to substantial transfers of employment to low-cost areas. Today, through satellites, you can remain in constant contact with offices in distant lands. This means that companies employing large back offices can close them and shift employment to any other part of the world. Swissair has recently transferred a significant part of its accounts department to India.

Still, certain services cannot be transferred overseas, such as health and education.

Indeed, but let's think that through to its practical conclusion. A nation's economy is split into two broad segments, one which produces wealth and the other which dispenses it. That in no way means that the latter is inferior; it includes such vital activities as health and education. Despite the fact that both kinds of activities are measured by GNP, one cannot reduce that part of our economy which produces wealth and expect to be able to maintain the other part which dispenses it. You must earn what you spend.

Presumably, the exchange rates between various currencies also have a substantial impact on the power to compete.

Of course. When Ricardo calculated comparative advantage, he did so in money terms. If a product costs X French francs in France and Y US dollars in America, all you need to do is to convert dollars into francs at the going rate of exchange and it will be clear where the advantage lies. In other words, the nation in which the product is cheaper is the nation that has the comparative advantage.

But this calculation can be brutally and suddenly transformed by a devaluation or a revaluation of one of the currencies. In 1981, one dollar was worth 4.25

French francs; by 1985, the dollar had risen sharply and was worth 10 French francs; by 1992, it had fallen again and was worth only 4.80 French francs. So take a product which in 1981 had the same cost whether manufactured in America or in France. Four years later, in 1985, it became more than twice as expensive in America as in France. This was no more than a reflection of the changing value of the dollar relative to the franc. Yet, according to Ricardo, each nation is supposed to specialize in those products in which it has a comparative advantage. If you followed this reasoning, industries on which you might have concentrated in America in 1981 would have had to be abandoned in 1985. And the reason would have been that the comparative advantage would have disappeared purely for monetary reasons. Then as the dollar fell again in 1992, the theory would have required that you recreate the industry in the United States. This is obvious nonsense. No one should sacrifice and recreate industries merely to be in rhythm with fluctuations in exchange rates.

Of course, those who believe in global free trade reject your arguments. In the first place, they cite the joint study published by the OECD and the World Bank which states that the application of the GATT proposals would increase world income by 213 billion dollars a year.[9] How can we turn down such growth?

If you study the reports, you will find that the increase is forecast to come about in ten years' time. Yes, 213 billion dollars is a large sum of money, but to assess its significance you must compare it to the world's GNP as it is forecast to be in ten years' time. 213 billion dollars represents no more than 0.7 per cent.[10] What is more, the General Secretary of the OECD described the report as being 'highly theoretical'.

It is also claimed that global free trade means that consumers will benefit from being able to buy cheaper imported products manufactured with low-cost labour.

Consumers are not just people who buy products, they are the same people who earn a living by working, and who pay taxes. As consumers they may be able to buy certain products more cheaply, although when Nike moved its manufacturing from the US to Asia, shoe prices did not drop. Instead profit margins rose. But the real cost to consumers of cheaper goods will be that they will lose their jobs, get paid less for their work and have to face higher taxes to cover the social cost of increased unemployment. Consumers are also citizens, many of whom live in towns. As unemployment rises and poverty increases, towns and cities will grow even more unstable. So the benefits of cheap imported products will be heavily outweighed by the social and economic costs they bring with them.

THE NEW UTOPIA:

*I understand your argument about increased
unemployment, but why should earnings be reduced?*

According to figures published by the US Department of
Labor,[11] since 1973 real hourly and weekly earnings, in
inflation-adjusted dollars, have already dropped
respectively by 13.4 per cent and 19.2 per cent, and that
was before the most recent GATT negotiations known as
the Uruguay Round. If 4 billion people enter the same
world market for labour and offer their work at a fraction
of the price paid to people in the developed world, it is
obvious that such a massive increase in supply will
reduce the value of labour. Also, organized labour will
lose practically all its negotiating power. When trade
unions ask for concessions, the answer will be: If you put
too much pressure on us, we will move offshore where we
can get much cheaper labour, which does not seek job
protection, long holidays, and all the other items that you
want to negotiate.

Global free trade will shatter the way in which value-
added is shared between capital and labour. Value-added
is the increase of value obtained when you convert raw
materials into a manufactured product. In mature
societies, we have been able to develop a general
agreement as to how it should be shared. That agreement
has been reached through generations of political debate,
elections, strikes, lockouts and other conflicts. Overnight
that agreement will be destroyed by the arrival of huge
populations willing to undercut radically the salaries

earned by our workforces. The social divisions that this will cause will be deeper than anything ever envisaged by Marx.

It is interesting to note that many US economists believe that the inflationary forces which normally follow a period of lax monetary policy will not occur in the same way on this occasion. They believe that the continued lowering of earnings resulting from global free trade, including the first effects of NAFTA (the North American Free Trade Agreement, which created an open market between Mexico, the US and Canada), will restrain inflation despite the fact that the Federal Reserve has maintained a loose monetary policy for one of the longest periods on record. In other words, the workforce will bear the brunt of the consequences of a prolonged policy of easy money by accepting reduced earnings to compensate for its inevitable inflationary effects.

Who will be the losers and who will be the winners under a system of global free trade?

The losers will, of course, be those people who become unemployed as a result of production being moved to low-cost areas. There will also be those who lose their jobs because their employers do not move offshore and are not able to compete with cheap imported products. Finally, there will be those whose earning capacity is reduced following the shift in the sharing of value-added away from labour.

THE NEW UTOPIA:

The winners will be those who can benefit from an almost inexhaustible supply of very cheap labour. They will be the companies who move their production offshore to low-cost areas; the companies who can pay lower salaries at home; and those who have capital to invest where labour is cheapest, and who as a result will receive larger dividends. But they will be like the winners of a poker game on the *Titanic*. The wounds inflicted on their societies will be too deep, and brutal consequences could follow.

The new phenomenon of our age is the emergence of transnational corporations, with the ability to move production at will anywhere in the world, in order to systematically benefit from lower wages wherever they are to be found. Transnational corporations now account for one-third of global output; their global annual sales have reached 4.8 trillion dollars, which is greater than total international trade. The largest 100 multinational corporations control about one-third of all foreign direct investment.[12] The globalization of the market is vital to them, both to produce cheaply and to sell universally. Because they do not necessarily owe allegiance to the countries where they operate, there is a divorce between the interests of the transnational corporations and those of society.

You must remember that one of the characteristics of developing countries is that a small handful of people controls the overwhelming majority of the nation's resources. It is these people who own most of their nation's industrial, commercial and financial enterprises and who assemble the cheap labour which is used to manufacture products for the developed world. Thus, it is the poor in the rich countries who will subsidize the rich in the poor countries. This will have a serious impact on the social cohesion of nations.

What are your thoughts about the World Trade Organization?

That is the organization which is supposed to replace GATT, regulate international trade, and lead us to global economic integration. It is yet another international bureaucracy whose functionaries will be largely autonomous. They report to over 120 nations and therefore, in practice, to nobody. Each nation will have one vote out of 120. Thus, America and every European nation will be handing over ultimate control of its economy to an unelected, uncontrolled, group of international bureaucrats.

Don't the developed nations have a moral responsibility to open their markets to the third world?

Let me start by quoting from a report by Herman Daly and Robert Goodland, published by the World Bank.

If by wise policy or blind luck, a country has managed to control its population growth, provide social insurance, high wages, reasonable working hours and other benefits to its working class (i.e. most of its citizens), should it allow these benefits to be competed down to the world average by unregulated trade? . . . This levelling of wages will be overwhelmingly downward due to the vast number and rapid growth rate of under-employed populations in the third world. Northern labourers will get poorer, while Southern labourers will stay much the same.[13]

But the application of GATT will also cause a great tragedy in the third world. Modern economists believe that an efficient agriculture is one that produces the maximum amount of food for the minimum cost, using the least number of people. That is bad economics. When you intensify the methods of agriculture and substantially reduce the number of people employed on the land, those who become redundant are forced into the cities. Everywhere you travel in the world you see those terrible slums made up of people who have been uprooted from the land. But, of course, the hurt is deeper. Throughout the third world, families are broken, the countryside is deserted, and social stability is destroyed. This is how the slums in Brazil, known as *favelas*, came into existence.

It is estimated that there are still 3.1 billion people in the world who live from the land. If GATT manages to impose worldwide the sort of productivity achieved by the intensive agriculture of nations such as Australia, then it is easy to calculate that about 2 billion of these people will become redundant. Some of these GATT refugees will move to urban slums. But a large number of them will be forced into mass migration. Today, as we discuss these issues, there is great concern about the 2 million refugees who have been forced to flee the tragic events in Rwanda. GATT, if it 'succeeds', will create mass migrations of refugees on a scale a thousand times greater. We will have profoundly and tragically destabilized the world's population.

But why do third world nations themselves support global free trade?

We must distinguish between the populations on the one hand and their ruling elites on the other. It is the elites who are in favour of global free trade. It is they who will be enriched. In India there have been demonstrations of up to one million people opposing the destruction of their rural communities, their culture and their traditions. In the Philippines several hundred thousand farmers protested against GATT because it would destroy their system of agriculture.

Vandana Shiva is an eminent Indian philosopher and physicist. She is Director of the Research Foundation for Science, Technology and National Resource Policy, and is the Science and Environment Adviser of the Third World Network. In India, she says, global free trade 'will mean a further destruction of our communities, uprooting of millions of small peasants from the land, and their migration into the slums of overcrowded cities. GATT destroys the cultural diversity and social stability of our nation . . . GATT, for us, implies recolonization.'[14]

Without global free trade, how could the developing nations emerge?

Those who wish to industrialize should form free trade areas, such as the trading regions currently being created in Latin America and South-East Asia. These areas should consist of nations with economies which are reasonably similar in terms of development and wage structures. Trading regions would enter into mutually beneficial bilateral agreements with other regions in the world. Freedom to transfer technology and capital would be maintained. Thus commercial organizations wishing to sell their products in any particular region would have to produce locally, importing capital and technology, and creating local employment and development. That is the way to create prosperity and stability in the developing world without destroying our own.

Some would say that Europe's employment problem is not GATT, but just the result of the old-fashioned diseases that one finds in uncompetitive, inflexible and spoiled societies. The welfare state is out of control; social costs borne by employers discourage the creation of new jobs; high government expenditure and taxation stifle the economy; state intervention is paralyzing; corporatism blocks remedial action, etc. Is that not true?

It is partially true, and those diseases must be treated

forcefully. But even if the treatment is successful, it will not solve the problems created by global free trade. Imagine that we were able to reduce at a stroke social charges and taxation so as to diminish the cost of labour by a full third. All it would mean is that instead of being able to employ forty-seven Vietnamese or forty-seven Filipinos for the price of one Frenchman, you could employ only thirty-one.

In any case, as we have already discussed, you must remember the example of France, where, over the past twenty years, spectacular growth in GNP has been surpassed by an even more spectacular rise in unemployment. This has taken place while Europe has progressively opened its market to international free trade. How can we accept a system which increases unemployment from 420,000 to 5.1 million during a period in which the economy has grown by 80 per cent?

You must understand that we are not talking about normal competition between nations. The 4 billion people who are joining the world economy have been part of a wholly different society, indeed, a different world. It is absurd to believe that suddenly we can create a global free trade area, a common market with, for example, China, without massive changes leading to consequences that we cannot anticipate.

Why is it not possible to repeat our successes in enriching countries like Taiwan, Hong Kong, South Korea and Singapore?

THE NEW UTOPIA:

The combined population of those countries is about 75 million people, so the scale of the problem is quite different. The US might be able to achieve a similar success with Mexico and, progressively, Western Europe could accommodate Eastern Europe. But attempting to integrate 4 billion people at once is blind utopianism.

In any case, each of those countries was a beneficiary of the Cold War. During that period, one or other of the superpowers sought to bring every part of the world into its camp. If one failed to fill the void, the other stepped in. That is why very favourable economic treatment was granted by the West to South Korea after the Korean War, and to Taiwan, Singapore and Hong Kong while China was considered a major communist threat.

Special economic concessions combined with their cheap and skilled labour forces made them successful. Over the past thirty years the balance of trade between these countries and the West has resulted in a transfer of tens of billions of dollars from us to them. The West has been haemorrhaging jobs and capital so as to help make them rich.

What do you recommend?

We must start by rejecting the concept of global free trade and we must replace it by regional free trade. That does not mean closing off any region from trading with the rest of the world. It means that each region is free to decide whether or not to enter into bilateral agreements with other regions. We must not simply open our markets to any and every product regardless of whether it benefits our economy, destroys our employment or destabilizes our society.

Does that not mean that we will cut ourselves off from innovation in other parts of the world?

No. Freedom of movement of capital should be maintained. If a Japanese or a European company wishes to sell its products in North America, it should invest in America. It should bring its capital and its technology, build factories in America, employ American people and become a corporate citizen of America. The same is true for American and Japanese firms wishing to sell their products in Europe.

Think about the difference between the GATT proposals and those I have just outlined. GATT makes it almost imperative for enterprises in the developed world to close down their production, eliminate their employees and move their factories to low-cost labour areas. What I am suggesting is the reverse: that to gain access to our markets foreign corporations would have to build factories, employ our people and contribute to our economies. It is the difference between life and death.

But won't that reduce competition?

Competition is an economic tool which is necessary to

promote efficiency, to apply downward pressure on prices and to stimulate innovation, diversity and choice. Vigorous competition needs a free market that is large and in which cartels and other limitations on competitive forces are forbidden. Europe and NAFTA are economically the two largest free trade areas ever created in history. Both are more than big enough to ensure highly competitive internal markets. They are vast and open and free and welcoming to innovations from anywhere in the world. Every significant corporation worldwide would have to come and compete, because no corporation could afford to bypass them – their markets are much too big and prosperous. But such competition would be constructive, not destructive.

Many will answer you by saying that you cannot export to other regions if you maintain a regional economy. There would be retaliation.

Take a look at Japan: the Japanese have certainly been able to export over the decades during which they protected their economy. In any case, bilateral trade agreements would allow for the exchange of products in a way which suited all parties. And our corporations would be free to invest and compete throughout the world.

What other recommendations do you have?

I totally reject the concept of specialization. Specializing in certain activities automatically means abandoning others. But one of the most valuable elements of our national patrimony is the existing complex of small and medium-sized businesses and craftsmen covering a wide range of activities. A healthy economy must be built like a pyramid. At the peak are the large corporations. At the base is the diversity of small enterprises. An economy founded on a few specialized corporations can produce large profits, but because the purpose of specialization is to streamline production, it cannot supply the employment which naturally results from a broadly diversified economy. Only a diversified economy is able to supply the jobs which can allow people to participate fully in society.

It is extraordinary to read economists commenting on the state of the nation. They believe that the profits of large corporations and the level of the stock markets are a reliable guide to the health of society and the economy. A healthy economy does not exclude from active participation a substantial proportion of its citizens.

You face a difficult problem in converting the British to these ideas. Britain has a long tradition of almost unconditional belief in free trade.

The origin of Britain's belief in free trade goes back to the early nineteenth century. It was in Britain, at that time, that the Industrial Revolution was born. The new industrial barons, whose power was growing in step with the expansion of British industry, needed ample and low-cost labour to populate their factories. The idea was that by importing cheap food from the colonies, British farms would be unable to compete. This would result in an exodus of farm workers to the cities. At that time, 80 per cent of the British population lived outside urban areas.[15] Once the farmers who had lost their livelihood reached the towns, they could be employed cheaply because cheap food was available from the colonies. What is more, the money that left Britain to buy the cheap food was recycled back to Britain to buy manufactured goods. At the time, Britain had a quasi-monopoly of manufacturing. Those were the dynamics which led to the repeal of the Corn Laws, which protected British agriculture, in 1846.

Today the circumstances are precisely reversed. Now only 1.1 per cent of the British workforce is employed in agriculture;[16] instead of a need for labour in the towns, there is chronic unemployment; and the money that leaves Britain to pay for imports no longer returns to buy British manufactured products. It goes to Japan or Korea or anywhere else in the world. The result is that Britain has a trade deficit in practically every major category of manufactured goods. And even though some of the large companies make good profits, 25 per cent of all households and nearly one child in three live in poverty.[17]

One of the greatest fallacies in economic thinking is that the funds that flow away from a nation as a result of a negative balance of trade, or of capital outflows, will automatically be recycled. Many economists belive that if, for example, the countries of Asia export more than they import, the excess cash will be invested abroad and ultimately this inflow will equal the outflow suffered by those with a trade deficit. Their assumption appears to be that for strictly mathematical reasons a nation's accounts must balance. But when a foreign nation does direct its excess cash to a nation suffering a deficit, that money usually returns in the form of investments in assets or in fixed-interest debt. Those assets thereby become the property of a foreign owner and their earnings flow to that owner. To illustrate the consequences, imagine a game of poker in which you lose more cash than you possess. Instead of paying in cash, you hand over ownership of your house and you continue to live in it as a tenant paying rent. Are we seriously to believe that such a transaction has had a nil effect on your financial position?

The US is now starting to suffer from this very problem. The *Economist* writes: 'Since 1981, America has shifted from being the world's biggest creditor to its biggest debtor, thanks to its persistent current account deficits. At the end of 1993, America had net foreign-debt obligations of $556 billion.'[18] And the *Washington Post* in an editorial, explains: 'Now the American economy has begun to pay out more in earnings on foreign investments at home, and on the country's huge accumulation of foreign debt, than it is earning on American investments abroad. It's the cost of running those big trade deficits year after year. They are being financed by foreign capital, and like any debtor country, the United States has to pay for the use of the money . . . Note that the American economy is now borrowing abroad to pay interest on its earlier foreign borrowings. That is no healthier for a country than it is for a business or a household. And how long can it go on? As long as foreigners are willing to lend. If and when their willingness diminishes, you will see it in higher interest rates. Should that happen, Americans would, as the economists say, have to adjust. That, as the Latin American debtor countries can testify, means a lower standard of living. The longer the foreign deficits pile up, the harder that adjustment will be.'[19]

In any case when funds leave a nation, those who receive them are free to invest anywhere in the world. And they will invest wherever the anticipated returns are highest. They will not necessarily choose societies which are bleeding to death.

When a system is valid in one set of circumstances, it is extremely unlikely to be valid in diametrically opposite circumstances. One would hope that this observation alone might prompt the British political elites to reassess their economic doctrine with an open mind.

We seem to have forgotten the purpose of the economy. The present British government is proud of the fact that labour costs less in Britain than in other European countries. But it does not yet understand that in a system of global free trade its competitors will no longer be in

Europe but in the low-cost countries. And compared to labour in those countries, Britain's labour will remain uncompetitive no matter how deeply the British government decides to impoverish its people.

In the great days of the USA, Henry Ford stated that he wanted to pay high wages to his employees so that they could become his customers and buy his cars. Today we are proud of the fact that we pay low wages. We have forgotten that the economy is a tool to serve the needs of society, and not the reverse. The ultimate purpose of the economy is to create prosperity with stability.

What do you mean by stability?

Stability does not mean ossification or standing still. A stable society can accommodate necessary change without social breakdown. A stable society can benefit from responsible economic growth without destroying itself.

How would you convince Germany of the merits of regional trade in view of the German elites' commitment to globalism?

The Germans should understand that by far their largest customers are their neighbours; about 70 per cent of Germany's exports are sold within Europe. Germany cannot want to see its principal customers impoverished as a result of haemorrhaging jobs and capital. German prosperity depends on the prosperity of the other nations of Europe; Germany's social stability will be deeply influenced by that of its neighbours; and, no matter how advanced its industrial skills, Germany will suffer from the transfer of production to low-cost areas, just like the rest of the developed world. What is more, under GATT, Germany will have to share its residual markets with imports from Japan, Korea and others.

How would you sum up the effects of regional free trade?

Let us imagine that Europe returns to the original concept of the Treaty of Rome, which was the basis for the creation of the European Community. Economically, its purpose was to establish the largest free market in the world. Within Europe, there would be no tariffs, no barriers, and a free and competitive market. Trade with nations outside Europe would be subject to a single tariff. This concept was known as Community preference. In other words, priority would be given to European jobs and industry. About twenty years ago, quietly, the technocrats who run Europe started to alter this basic principle and move progressively towards international free trade. Ever since, unemployment in Europe has swollen despite growth in GNP. The Treaty of Maastricht enshrines this change and makes global free trade one of the fundamental principles on which the new Europe is to be built.

If we were to return to the ideas of our founding fathers and reimpose Community preference, overnight all the enterprises which have moved their production to low-cost countries would have to return. They could no longer competitively import products manufactured outside Europe. Factories would be built, Europeans would be employed, the economy would prosper and social stability would return. What is more, international corporations wishing to sell their products within Europe would also have to build, employ and participate in the European economy. From being a community which, at the moment, reeks of death, it would all of a sudden become one of the most exciting places in which to invest and participate. And European corporations would go out to invest and contribute to the prosperity of regions throughout the world. The same is true for North America.

Insofar as free trade areas consisting of developing economies are concerned, they also would prosper. For example, currently free trade areas are being formed in Latin America and in South-East Asia. Most North American, European and Japanese corporations will wish to sell their products in these large markets. To do so, they will have to transfer capital and technology, build factories in Latin America and South-East Asia and employ Latin Americans and Asians. By participating in these economies, they would encourage development.

GATT must be rejected. It is too profoundly flawed to be a stepping stone to a better system. The damage it will inflict on the communities of both the developed world and the third world will be intolerable.

THE NEW UTOPIA:

1. Ricardo, D., *On the Principles of Political Economy and Taxation*, London: J.M. Dent and Sons, 1992.

2. World Bank, *World Population Projections: 1994-95 Edition*, Baltimore: Johns Hopkins University Press for The World Bank, August 1994.

3. In Borotra, F., *Rapport de la commission d'enquête de l'Assemblée nationale sur les délocalisations à l'étranger d'activités économiques*, Paris: Journal Officiel, 2 December 1993.

4. 'IBM is Overhauling Disk Drive Business, Cutting Jobs, Shifting Production to Asia', *Wall Street Journal*, New York, 5 August 1994.

5. 'Boeing to Expand China Operations, Names New President for Unit There', *Wall Street Journal*, New York, 9 August 1994.

6. 'US Multinationals take "Brain Work" to Plants Overseas', *Wall Street Journal Europe,* 30 September 1994.

7. 'Le TGV Seoul Pusan', *Le Figaro*, Paris, 19 April 1994; 'Industrie choisie de préférence à son concurrent Allemand, GEC Alsthom construira le TGV en Corée du Sud', *Le Monde*, Paris, 19 April 1994.

8. 'Industrie: Selon Henri Martre, président du GIFAS, la reprise dans l'aéronautique n'aura pas lieu avant 1995', *Le Monde*, Paris, 29 April 1993.

9. Goldin, I. and van der Mensbrugghe, D., *Trade Liberalization: What's at Stake*, Washington: World Bank and OECD, 1993.

10. 'Where Gatt's $200bn Really Comes From', *Financial Times*, London, 4 October 1993.

THE RESPONSE

11. US Department of Labor Bureau of Labor Statistics, *Business Establishment Survey*, average hourly and weekly earnings of production or non-supervisory workers in 1982 dollars, provided from on-line search, 12 August 1994.

12. 'Elite companies rule world of trade', *Guardian*, London, 31 August 1994.

13. Daly, H., and Goodland, R., *An Ecological-Economic Assessment of Deregulation of International Commerce under GATT*, Washington: World Bank, September 1992.

14. Interview on French television channel TFI, 11 June 1994, and personal communication.

15. Dyos, H., and Wolff, M., *The Victorian City*, London: Routledge, 1973.

16. Department of Employment, *Employment Gazette*, London, September 1994.

17. Government Statistical Service, *Households Below Average Income*, London: HMSO, 1994.

18. 'Financial Indicators', *The Economist*, London, 5 November 1994.

19. 'Paying for the Foreign Debts', *Washington Post*, final edition, 3 November 1994.